MARTIN
LUTHER

Faith in Christ and
the Gospel

MARTIN LUTHER

Faith in Christ and the Gospel

selected spiritual writings

introduced and edited by
Eric W. Gritsch

New City Press

Published in the United States by New City Press
202 Cardinal Rd., Hyde Park, NY 12538
©1996 New City Press

Cover painting: "Martin Luther" by Lucas Cranach (1528). Used with permission from Lutherhalle Wittenberg, Germany.

Library of Congress Cataloging-in-Publication Data:

Luther, Martin, 1483-1546
   [Selections. English. 1996]
   Faith in Christ and the Gospel : selected spiritual writings /
Martin Luther ; edited and introduced by Eric W. Gritsch.

   Includes bibliographical references.
   ISBN 1-56548-041-4 (pbk.)
   1. Spiritual life—Lutheran Church.   2. Lutheran Church—
Doctrines.   I. Title.
BR331.E5   1996
248.4'841—dc20   95-34532

Printed in the United States of America

Contents

Foreword

This book is in itself an eloquent witness to how far Lutherans and Catholics have advanced in their quest for mutual understanding on the way to their promised, hoped-for and imperative unity as fellow Christians. That a Catholic publishing house would engage one of our foremost Luther scholars to bring together a collection of Luther's writings for people today is something new and remarkable. Once in our hands, it seems so logical, needed and welcome.

Martin Luther, a towering figure who stood at the vortex of the sixteenth century storms that left Catholics and Protestants divided, is one who belongs to all of us. Certainly to Lutherans, who have kept his spirit and message alive. But also to Catholics. Every Roman Catholic knows his name; and most have heard the legendary account of his nailing "Ninety-five Theses" calling for reforms to the door of a church in 1517. The history of the Roman Catholic Church cannot be told without him. However we looked on him, as renegade or reformer, we knew he was one of ours.

Still, for all of that, it is true that few Roman Catholics have had immediate contact with the man through his writings and thus do not have a direct sense of him and his creativity. In part this was no doubt due to a defensiveness and aversion created by the bitterness of past divisions. But beyond that, without a guide it is hard to find one's way in approaching the monumental range of Luther's writings. The entire collection of his works fills over a hundred volumes. In Eric Gritsch we have one of the most experienced and expert of guides. The terrain he guides us through is one he has himself traversed for years.

What may strike many readers of this collection is the vivid freshness that comes off pages written in the sixteenth century. Their urgency, directness and simplicity seem to aim right at the reader of this century as if they were written today. To many of us that comes as a discovery, for in fact Luther was a late medieval Catholic wrestling with what he saw to be a spiritual crisis of the people of his time. As one can see, he was motivated by a strong pastoral sense. His purpose was to console and encourage people, to help them overcome anxiety. He strove to break the grip of "works righteousness," the idea that by what we do we can and must "earn" from God what is truly beyond us. Luther calls Christians to a free-fall reliance upon Christ through faith made possible by his mercy, grace and favor. This message remains relevant today. The times we live in are different from but not entirely dissimilar to Luther's. His was an age of the "anguished conscience" that could not find peace. Ours is an age troubled by a different form of "works righteousness," an achievement oriented society that strives for accomplishments but experiences a certain uncertainty or emptiness about the deeper meaning of our lives. In our time, too, our "works" can imprison our souls. Luther's call to faith, to confident and hope-filled reliance on the Lord still speaks directly to us, putting the liberating message of the gospel before us.

In this collection the figure of Luther emerges as a pastor, a teacher and preacher of the gospel. Agree with him or not on one matter or another, reading Luther is always invigorating. By all accounts he is incontestably a major Christian spiritual writer. Addressing the Lutheran World Federation in 1970, Cardinal Johannes Willebrands, president of Rome's Secretariat for Promoting Christian Unity, spoke of Martin Luther as "our common teacher" (a title otherwise used only in reference to Thomas Aquinas). Subsequently, on the five hundredth anniversary of Luther's birth (1993), the cardinal said in Leipzig, "Martin Luther is not only present in the life of Evangelical Christianity; he is equally present in the *oikoumene* of all Christendom. We must therefore re-read his theological legacy; above all we must re-read it together and participate in a critical learning process that complies with one of Luther's favorite quotations from Paul: 'Test everything; hold fast to what is good' (1 Thes 5:21)."

Eric Gritsch in this collection puts his finger on the pulse of the Reformer so that we can sense the heartbeat of this religious genius.

John F. Hotchkin
Executive Director, National Conference of Catholic Bishops
Secretariat for Ecumenical and Interreligious Affairs

Introduction

A Retrospective Reflection

> Make no reference to my name; let them [followers] call
> themselves Christians, not Lutherans. What is Luther?
> After all, the teaching is not mine. Neither was I cruci-
> fied for anyone. . . . Let us abolish all party names and
> call ourselves Christians, after him whose teaching we
> hold. (LW 45:70-71)

Luther penned these words in 1522, shortly after his condemnation by Church and state. It took some time to appreciate this
"catholic" Luther. Until the dawn of this century, he had been
portrayed as a hero by Protestants and as a villain by Catholics.
The edition of his voluminous works since 1883, the creation of
an International Congress for Lutheran Research in 1956, and the
Second Vatican Council (1962-65) have changed the black and
white images of Luther to an image reflecting the rich tradition of
the Church.[1] Luther knew that tradition well, and he tried to distill
from it what he thought might renew his Church, the Western
medieval Church led by the bishop of Rome.

The Lutheran World Federation, representing sixty million
Lutherans in its headquarters in Geneva, and the Secretariat for
Promoting Christian Unity in Rome have initiated intensive dia-
logues in the wake of the Second Vatican Council. The Lutheran-
Catholic dialogue in the United States is an impressive model of
this new relationship between Luther and the heirs of Rome.[2]

---

1. Eric W. Gritsch, "Luther: From Rejection to Rehabilitation" in H. George
   Anderson & James R. Crumley Jr. (eds.), *Promoting Unity. Themes in
   Lutheran-Catholic Dialogue.* Festschrift for Johannes Cardinal Willebrands
   (Minneapolis: Augsburg Fortress, 1989), 9-16.

2. *Lutherans and Catholics in Dialogue* I-VIII (Minneapolis: Augsburg, 1965-95).
   Topics include: 1. Nicene Creed, 2. Baptism, 3. Eucharist, 4. Ministry, 5. Papacy,
   6. Teaching Authority, 7. Justification By Faith, 8. Mary and the Saints, 9. Word
   of God: Scripture and Tradition.

This relationship is undergirded by a change in Catholic Luther studies since 1940, when the German Catholic historian Joseph Lortz published a revisionist history of the Reformation in Germany. He portrayed Luther as an exponent of a late medieval Catholic theological tradition which, however, did not fully represent the official teaching of the Church regarding salvation. But Lortz no longer viewed Luther as a heretic. Luther's struggle with the papacy disclosed "mutual misunderstanding on a grand scale."[3]

International Luther studies find Luther to be quite "catholic," and Catholics have become attracted to his ideas and praxis of spiritual formation. Cardinal Jan Willebrands called Luther "a teacher we have in common" (*gemeinsamer Lehrer*), because he taught "absolute trust and adoration of God."[4] Similar statements about Luther were made in commemoration of his five hundredth birthday in 1983. The international Roman Catholic/Lutheran Joint Commission called for a positive reception of Luther's concerns: his "call for Church reform," his "witness to the gospel," and his care for those "whose consciences suffered under the dominion of the law and human ordinances."[5]

Such views suggest that Luther has been rehabilitated to some degree by Roman Catholic authorities. Catholic theologians have certainly acknowledged Luther's wisdom as a source for Church renewal. For he may have anticipated and expressed experiences of faith that did not exist in his time. But they do now, given the reality of the contemporary world.[6]

In the light of these and other ways of looking back, Luther is a "father of the Church" rather than just a "heretic."

---

3. Joseph Lortz, *The Reformation in Germany*, tr. Ronald Walls (New York/London: Herder and Herder, 1968; first German edition 1939-40); German edition, 781.
4. Speech at the assembly of the Lutheran World Federation in 1970 in Evian, Switzerland. "Gesandt in die Welt," *Lutherische Rundschau* 20 (1970): 459.
5. *Facing Unity: Models, Forms and Phases of Catholic-Lutheran Fellowship* (Geneva: Lutheran World Federation, 1985), 72-79.
6. Otto H. Pesch, *Hinführung zu Luther* (Mainz: Matthias Grünewald Verlag, 1982), 273.

The Plight of a Churchman

Martin Luther (November 10, 1483 to February 18, 1546) was born into a restless time. "Renaissance," a rebirth of Christian art originating in Italy in the fourteenth century, and "Humanism," a subsequent focus on earthly human life advocated by universities, challenged the authority of the Western Church led by the papacy in Rome. Renaissance scholars and Humanists discovered a wealth of sources that did not seem to confirm some of the fundamental teachings of the Church, such as the apostolic succession of popes. This tradition had never been accepted by the Eastern Church, led by the patriarch of Constantinople since 1054, when divisive views on authority split Christendom into two communions. Moreover, papal power had been seriously curtailed by the rise of two competitive papacies, one in Rome and another in Avignon, France (1309 to 1415).

Medieval Christendom was also threatened by the rise of Islam, founded by Mohammed in 622. Terrorizing crusades against his followers had been unsuccessful, and Turkish armies moved as far as Vienna by 1529. They were finally forced to retreat to Southern Europe, where they established enduring strongholds.

Europe also became linked with the newly discovered lands across the oceans, such as the American continent claimed by Spain in 1492. The geographical discoveries confronted Europeans with new ways of thinking, trading, and life-styles. In addition, the invention of an efficient printing press by Johann Gutenberg in Mainz, Germany, radically changed communication. Printing ideas and money generated radically new views of life. New ideas could be quickly disseminated, and paper money made the Fugger Bank in Augsburg a significant partner in global trade.

But social structures prevailed. There was the secular nobility with its hierarchy of emperors, kings, and princes; and there was the spiritual nobility with its hierarchy of popes, bishops, and priests. In addition, the monastic life could be chosen as a special way to serve God. The common people, mostly peasants and traders, represented a state close to slavery; they were dominated by secular and spiritual nobility, the owners of territories.

Church and state increasingly engaged in power struggles. Cries for reform multiplied by the beginning of the sixteenth century. The Church tried to keep peace by urging people to repent of their sins through the sacrament of penance. Confessors often created fear in penitents by alerting them to the possibility of eternal punishment. There was much talk of purgatory as a place between heaven and hell, an opportunity to be cleansed by fire from the contagious plague of human sins.[7] Going to confession became the first step after infant baptism toward salvation mediated by the Church as the only legitimate agent of God.[8]

Young Luther embodied medieval spirituality. Born in the village of Eisleben, he was raised and educated by conservative parents, relatives, and tutors, destined by his father to become a lawyer. This was the popular way to get part of the fortune of the rich and noble. But the twenty-one-year-old law student became scared to death during a thunderstorm in the countryside. Well trained for emergencies he cried out, "Help Saint Anna [the grandmother of Jesus], and I will become a monk." She did and he did. He joined the Augustinian Hermits in Erfurt where he had previously studied law. He was a dedicated monk and did very good academic work. He earned the degree of Bachelor of Arts in 1502, the Master of Arts in 1505, and was ordained into the priesthood in 1507. His special relationship to the Bible earned him the Biblical Baccalaureate in 1509 at Wittenberg University. At the same time he also became Master of Sentences.[9] Regarded

---

7. How the sacrament of penance became significant has been shown by Thomas N. Tentler, *Sin and Confession on the Eve of the Reformation* (Princeton: Princeton University Press, 1977).

8. The Fourth Lateran Council in 1215 decreed that one had to be seven years old to confess and commune.

9. Based on intensive study and tests of the accepted textbook in medieval theology, Peter Lombard's *The Sentences (Sententiarium)*, 1154-57. The title *sententiarius* authorized Luther to teach at the university.

as a very reliable friar, Luther was sent to Rome in 1510 to ask for a judgment on a dispute over the matter of strict or relaxed application of rules; Luther favored the former, but Rome left the matter in the hands of the German Vicar General, Johann von Staupitz, who decided not to force a merger of the two groups. He appointed Luther subprior of the Wittenberg monastery, with primary responsibility of supervising academic studies.

The monk, priest, and teacher Luther continued to experience the spiritual trials that had driven him into the monastery. He was still afraid to die and to face an angry God in the afterlife. The Church constantly proclaimed such a God, and even Christ was portrayed as the judge of the end-time. Was there a gracious, loving God? How could Luther pacify his enduring "terrors of conscience"? He went to more oral confessions than any other friar in the monastery, always talking about his "spiritual trials" (*Anfechtungen* in German). Finally, Staupitz gave him a direct order: intensify your Bible work and earn a doctorate in biblical studies, the highest academic degree at the university. Luther obeyed and earned the doctorate in record time in 1512. A year later he was appointed to the Augustinian chair of biblical theology, previously occupied by Staupitz, who moved into retirement to Salzburg, Austria. Luther began to teach in 1513, offering lectures on Psalms, Romans (1515-16), and Galatians (1516-17).

When Luther worked with the interpretation of Romans 1:17 ("For in it [the gospel] the righteousness of God is revealed through faith for faith; as it is written, 'The one who is righteous will live by faith' [Hab 2:4])," he experienced a spiritual breakthrough. It was the rediscovery of what was to Luther the decisive sense of the Bible, namely, that one is right with God, "righteous" by trust or faith in what God did in Christ, rather than what any moral effort could do to appease the wrath of God against sinners. This insight made Luther feel like being "born again" and opened for him the gates of paradise.[10]

---

10. LW 34:337. Reasons and dates for Luther's breakthrough have been debated for a long time. The dating tended to be late, perhaps 1516-18. For the most recent

But this insight was not in conformity with existing doctrine and practice. The Church, to be sure, taught that personal faith was significant, but as faith in the truths promulgated by the Church. The Church taught that its moral mandates were part of the process of salvation. This process begins as cooperation between natural moral efforts (some work of charity) and the grace of God embodied in Jesus Christ; and this grace is made available in sacraments. So people were exhorted to do works of charity during the week and then come to Church for holy communion on Sunday. Human nature cooperated with divine grace. Luther denied any such cooperation, rejecting the sophisticated argumentation for it by Thomas Aquinas (1225-74). Steeped in the study of Augustine (354-430), Luther had become convinced that the power of sin prevented any moral effort to become good enough to cooperate with divine grace.

Luther experienced an abusive form of "justification" by good works when he began to hear confessions at one of the churches in Wittenberg. Penitents told him that they had done satisfaction for specific sins through the purchase of "indulgences," printed "permits" or coupons. Official doctrine defined an "indulgence" as a good work of moral effort on the part of a penitent. The priest would pronounce forgiveness to penitent sinners if they promised to make payments in terms of time, spiritual exercises, or with money. Then they could escape eternal punishment in hell or suffering in purgatory. The medium of printing led to a particular abuse of indulgences. The German bishop Albrecht of Mainz used the sale of indulgences to help pay debts to Rome. Rome advocated the sale to help build St. Peter's Church. The Fugger Bank in Augsburg even hired a Dominican monk, Johann Tetzel, to advertise and sell indulgences. He did so by using the slogan, "As soon as the coin in the coffer rings, the soul from purgatory springs." This slogan abused official doctrine, which permitted forgiveness of sins committed in this life, but not forgiveness in any phase of the

stance see Martin Brecht, *Martin Luther*, 3 vols., tr. James L. Schaaf (Minneapolis: Fortress, 1985-93), 1:221-36.

after-life. Tetzel, however, promised release of deceased relatives from purgatory through the purchase of an indulgence.

Luther opposed the abuse, first in sermons to parishioners, then by calling for an academic debate through the now famous Ninety-Five Theses of October 31, 1517 (LW 31:25-33). After they had been posted in Latin, they appeared in German copies almost everywhere. Cartoons heralded Luther as a God-sent reformer of Christendom. Cartoonists portrayed him as the German Hercules, who wrestled down his opponents including Thomas of Aquinas. He also was pictured as the scribe of the Saxon prince who paid his salary at Wittenberg University, Frederick, later called "the wise."

Since 1517 Luther was a public figure, praised by many, but also attacked by others, such as the Dominican indulgences seller Tetzel and Bishop Albrecht of Mainz. The bishop urged Rome to silence Luther. Rome requested that Prince Frederick do so. But he politely refused, counseling a hearing of Luther in Germany. Since Frederick was one of the seven powerful "electors" of the Holy Roman Emperor, Rome was careful not to offend him. Moreover, the election of a new Holy Roman Emperor was pending, since Maximilian I was dying.[11] Luther was in trouble. He had expected his Church to listen to a complaint about the abuse of indulgences. He also had hoped to draw other theologians into a debate about the norms of proper theology and Church practice. But instead he was faced with an ultimatum: be silent or be accused of heresy.

---

11. The election of a Holy Roman Emperor was regulated by the "golden bull" of 1356. Three ecclesiastical rulers (the archbishops of Mainz, Trier, and Cologne) and four secular princes (king of Bohemia, duke of Saxony, margrave of Brandenburg, and count of the Palatinate) were designated "electors." Previously, the emperor evolved through power politics, beginning with the coronation of Charlemagne, blessed by Pope Leo III in 800. When Maximilian died in 1518 the seven electors ended up in a tie vote, three favoring the election of Francis I of France and three favoring Charles I of Spain. Frederick broke the tie by voting for Charles I who became Emperor Charles V in 1519. From now on he would be careful not to offend Frederick. See Karl Brandi, *The Emperor Charles V*, tr. C. V. Wedgewood (New York: Jonathan Cape, 1965).

Undaunting Work for Renewal

Events took quick turns after the election of Emperor Charles V and Luther's public demands for a public hearing. Prince Frederick insisted that his now famous professor be dealt with in Germany rather than in Rome. Popular memory had not forgotten the fate of the Czech churchman John Huss, who had been promised a hearing by Rome, but was executed without a trial at the Council of Constance in 1415. Prince Frederick persuaded Cardinal Cajetan to meet with Luther in Augsburg in 1518, where a German assembly of princes, called "diet," was to meet. The cardinal refused to debate with Luther and dismissed him as a potential heretic.

While Rome investigated Luther for heresy, he succeeded to be part of a scholarly debate in Leipzig in 1519. The debate had been arranged by German politicians, who asked the well-known Dominican official Johann Eck to oppose Luther. Eck did so in writing before the debate. Luther responded by highlighting what would become the controversial thesis of the debate, thesis thirteen: whether the papacy was of divine origin, as claimed by Rome, or a human institution signaling an earthly Christian unity. Luther defended the latter point of view, stressing that there had not been a pope in charge of the Church in the first five hundred years of Christianity. Eck declined any consideration and accused Luther of reviving the teachings of Huss, who had made the same claims. When Luther openly sided with Huss, the debate was interrupted by its umpires. After some time, Luther was declared the loser by the theological faculties who had served as umpires, among them the University of Paris and Luther's own alma mater, the University of Erfurt. But he had won broad support among a great multitude of people in favor of radical Church reform, many of them powerful politicians and intellectuals.

By 1521, both Church and state had condemned Luther. A papal bull (so called because the seal is known as *bulla*) called Luther a "boar in the vineyard of the Lord," and the edict of Worms branded him as a dangerous demagogue. Luther probably had his finest hour at the assembly in Worms where he answered the question, "Do you recant?" with the statement that discloses the norms by which he wished to be judged:

> Unless I am convinced by the testimony of the *Scriptures* or by clear reason . . . I am bound by the Scriptures . . . and my *conscience* is captive to the *word of God*. I cannot and will not retract anything, since it is neither safe nor right to go against conscience. I cannot do otherwise, here I stand, may God help me. Amen.[12]

At issue were the meaning of the Bible as the vessel of the word of God, reason used as a tool to interpret scripture and tradition, and conscience as a barometer of personal commitment. Luther used these norms to establish what he thought would be the essential components of Christianity: the incarnation of the triune God in Jesus; trust in Jesus alone as the only source of salvation from sin; the word of scripture and two sacraments derived from it (baptism and eucharist); and the Church as the communion of the faithful called to attest God's love for the world in word and deed, indeed by martyrdom if necessary. Luther had made his position clear in four treatises in 1520.[13] But the chief issue was the nature and function of the final authority in the Church, called "teaching office" (*magisterium*).

Frederick the Wise protected Luther from possible persecution by concealing him in one of his castles, the Wartburg, where Luther stayed for almost a year. Only Luther's close friends knew of his whereabouts. When people in Wittenberg became restless, agitated by radicals who predicted doom and even the end of the world, Luther returned and helped establish law and

---

12. LW 32:112-13. There is some doubt whether Luther said, "I cannot do otherwise, here I stand, May God help me." Not all eyewitness accounts have the longer versions. But Luther's own account includes this version. Italics added.

13. *The Freedom of the Christian* (LW 31:333-77); *To the Christian Nobility of the German Nation Concerning the Reform of the Christian Estate* (LW 36:11-126); *Treatise on Good Works* (LW 44:21-114); *The Babylonian Captivity of the Church* (LW 36:11-126).

order. But he also wanted to make the small town of Wittenberg (less than three thousand inhabitants) a model of renewal. In 1523 he initiated a program for reforming worship and education. The liturgy of the Mass was carefully revised and worship services were more often conducted in German than in Latin. Luther taught that all the baptized participate in God's ministry; they were to do so in public worship by singing, reading biblical lessons, and in the collection of gifts. Financial offerings were used to curb poverty. Money was put in a "common chest" whose contents were guarded and distributed by trustworthy laymen. Luther also produced two popular catechisms in 1529, a "small" one for the young, and a "large" one for adults. Luther wrote them with the premise that every family would constitute a catechetical unit, cooperating with religious instruction in schools.

The success of the "Lutherans" (a nickname imposed by opponents) compelled Emperor Charles V to call for an assembly of princes in Augsburg "to hear everyone's opinion," as he put it in the invitation. The young reform movement decided to submit a "confession of faith" in two parts: first, to indicate how Luther's reform proposals amplify or reduce what the Church officially believed; and second, to list items which could be reasonably negotiated, such as the marriage of priests and the rationale for monasticism. Luther's young colleague and friend, Philip Melanchthon, drafted the confession, later known as the *Augsburg Confession* of 1530. Emperor Charles V immediately called together a group of theologians in order to refute the confession. The refutation was entitled *Confutation* and had no official approval by Rome. Since powerful princes supported the Lutheran confession, Charles V postponed any punitive action against schismatics. He also called on Rome to settle theological questions in a council of bishops, chaired by the pope; such "general" or "ecumenical' councils had become the teaching authority in the Roman Catholic Church.

The threat of a new Turkish invasion from the South, the power of Lutheran territories (which included Scandinavia since 1536), and the spread of reforming ideas throughout Europe (especially in Switzerland through Ulrich Zwingli and John Calvin who had disciples in France and England) endangered the unity of Christendom in the West. Many political leaders no longer expected much leadership either from the emperor or the pope. That is why they banded together in military alliances. Catholic princes formed a "holy league" and Lutherans responded with a defense league formed at Smalcald, Saxony. By 1537 religious war seemed imminent. Lutheran princes asked Luther to draft a statement, summarizing his teaching so that they would know what to die for. Luther, gravely ill with angina pectoris, kidney and gall stones, drafted the *Smalcald Articles* of 1537. They focused on Luther's conviction, based on the Bible, that everything in life and death must be grounded in absolute trust in Christ who "was put to death for our trespasses and raised again for our justification" (Rom 4:25). "Nothing in this article can be given up or compromised," Luther wrote, "even if heaven and earth and things temporal should be destroyed" (BC 292:5).

When Luther quickly recovered from his various illnesses in 1537, he withdrew to Wittenberg where he was free to continue his teaching. Teaching the Bible was his favorite activity. He worked on a massive commentary on Genesis, dealt with various aspects of social and political life, such as economic justice (tracts against usury), war and peace (advocating a just war of self-defense over against an unjust war of aggression) and the question of the conversion of the Jews. He probably created the darkest hour of his career with his attack against the Jews who refused to convert. Originally friendly with them and tolerant, Luther penned a treatise in 1543, entitled *On the Jews and Their Lies*. In it he called for their expulsion from Christian territories, for labor camps if they refused to leave, and for withdrawing all civil rights from them. Luther based this judgment on the theological theory that God had withdrawn from the Jews because they killed Jesus, and therefore Christians too must rid themselves of them. Luther accepted a crude antisemitism which, in its medieval form, was laced with superstition (Jews killed babies, poisoned wells, and were secret agents of the devil).[14]

Luther died in his native town Eisleben in the early morning hours of February 18, 1546. Probable cause of death was a heart attack. At the time of his death he was surrounded by three sons and two friends who had been with him during his negotiations with two local nobles to help settle their controversy over property. Luther settled the matter to their satisfaction. Shortly after his death, a note was found on his working desk with reflections about the interpretation of the Bible. No one can understand Roman authors about agriculture, Luther had written, without being a farmer for five years. The same is true for understanding the Bible. As Luther put it: "Let nobody suppose that he [*sic.*] tasted the holy scriptures sufficiently unless he has ruled over the Churches with the prophets for a hundred years. We are all beggars. That is true" (LW 54:476).

The Lutheran Smalcald League was defeated in battle in 1547 after a brief war. The final peace treaty of Augsburg in 1555 decided that Lutheran princes had the right to adhere to the Augsburg Confession of 1530, and Catholic princes could maintain the old religion in their territories. Rome finally responded to Lutheranism and other reform movements with the decrees of the Council of Trent (1545-63 with interruptions). The Council reformed much that was wrong, especially abuses in doctrine and morals. But it condemned what Luther had affirmed as his last will and testament at Smalcald in 1537: "justification by faith." It is an irony of history, or a clue of divine providence, that the Lutheran-Catholic Dialogue in the United States reported an agreement on "justification" echoing Luther's language in a "fundamental affirmation" of faith in Christ alone.[15]

---

14. Text of the treatise in LW 47:137-306. On the issue of Luther and antisemitism see Eric W. Gritsch, "Luther and the Jews: Toward a Judgment of History" in Harold H. Ditmanson (ed.), *Stepping-Stones to Further Jewish-Lutheran Relationships. Key Lutheran Statements* (Minneapolis: Augsburg, 1990), 104-19.

15. *Lutherans and Catholics in Dialogue VII: Justification by Faith,* H. George Anderson, T. Austin Murphy, Joseph A, Burgess, eds. (Minneapolis: Augsburg, 1985), 72:157.

That agreement was possible because of the Catholic renewal generated by the Second Vatican Council. This renewal was based on the rediscovery of the power of the word of God explicated in 1965 (*Dei Verbum*),[16] on the four hundredth anniversary of the conclusion of the Council of Trent. The agreement on justification by faith was made in 1983, the five hundredth anniversary of Luther's birth.

The Man and His Work

Luther was a robust man, of peasant stock, shaped by monastic habits that made him a workaholic when he left the monastery. He used the monastic discipline of little sleep and spiritual concentration to do an incredible amount of work within three decades (1516-46). His literary legacy is staggering: about 450 treatises, some of them quite voluminous; 2,600 letters; more than 3,000 sermons; but above all, lengthy commentaries on the Bible (30 volumes in the American edition of his works—12 of them on the Book of Genesis). The German and Latin Weimar Edition consists of more than 100 oversized volumes. Luther admitted being verbose. But he did not take his literary production as seriously as authors usually do. "I wished that all my books were buried in perpetual oblivion," he prefaced a 1545 edition of his Latin works, "so that there might be room for better ones" (LW 34:327). In any case, Luther's literary legacy launched avalanches of studies about him ever since his death, but increasingly in this century. There is an almost unfathomable "Lutherania," ranging from detailed studies of brief texts to audacious psychotherapeutic analyses of his mind.[17]

Luther was above all a Bible scholar. The Bible disclosed to

---

16. *Vatican II. The Conciliar and Post-Conciliar Documents,* ed. Austin Flannery (Northport: Costello Publishing Company, 1975), 750-65.

17. A typical example is the treatment by Erik H. Erikson, *Young Man Luther* (New York: Horton, 1958). It is based on unreliable "table talks" without regard for solid historical evidence in Luther's correspondence. For a detailed analysis of this treatment see Eric W. Gritsch, *Martin—God's Court Jester. Luther in Retrospect,* 2d. ed. (Ramsey: Sigler Press, 1991), 148-52.

him a wonderful God who is in love with the world, despite the human sin of rebellion against the Creator. He studied the story of Israel, with all its ups and downs, filled with human tragedy and human happiness. All of history aims at God's incarnation in Christ, as Luther learned from Paul (Gal 4:4). Luther shared with Paul the sense of the imminent second coming of Christ at the end of time. He saw visible signs of the end: the aches and pains of a bureaucratic Church; the radical spirits of those who wanted to feel God only mystically, without any external signs like word and sacrament; the Turks who seemed to have become the divine whip for hypocritical Christians. And yet, Luther still sensed the joys and wonders of divine creation. When his first son was born, he marveled at the mystery of birth. "Katie" (Katharina von Bora) was twenty-six when she married Luther who was forty-two. She was of noble birth and fled the nunnery in 1525 to meet Luther. They had six children and took in four more from relatives after they had moved into the Augustinian cloister in Wittenberg, a wedding gift of Frederick the Wise in 1525. Its many rooms were filled with the sounds of prayer, music, laughter, and table talk. Famous people came to visit Luther even after he had been declared an outlaw in the Holy Roman Empire.

Lean and gaunt before his condemnation in 1521, and increasingly obese thereafter, Luther always had a busy day, teaching, writing, preaching, counseling, praying, singing, and playing with the family. He loved music which "deserves the highest praise, next to the word of God [because] she serves to cast out Satan" (LW 53:323). He designated himself as a "court jester," that ancient figure who appears in foolish clothes, usually riding a donkey, offering advice and criticism to governments. That is how Luther introduced himself to the German nobles in 1520, when he asked them to serve as "emergency bishops" in the face of the Church's crisis of leadership (LW 44:123-24). Knowing fully well that good princes are "rare birds," he nevertheless called on them to exercise leadership in the Church as baptized Christians who have a Christian vocation.

Luther was a wordsmith who could outdo almost any opponent in argumentation, wit, and polemics. The sixteenth century was a violent age. Violent language was an integral part of that age. Humanists, theologians, politicians, and others at the top of society enjoyed "muck." As the mild-mannered, popular Luther biographer Roland H. Bainton put it: "Luther delighted less in muck than many of the literary men of his age; but if he did indulge, he excelled in this as in every other area of speech."[18] Psychoanalysts have tried to pin Luther down in the strange realm of mental illness. But the historical evidence is against them. Luther maintained a steady rhythm of work, even while suffering from kidney stone attacks and other physical illnesses.[19] Like his model Paul, he felt the foolishness of being made strong in weakness (2 Cor 11:21b, 30).

Luther is a formidable figure in the Christian tradition. He was an expert biblical scholar concerned about the proper distinction between the word of God and human authority. He rediscovered the power of sin as idolatry—the ever-present desire to be like God (Gen 3:5)— and the force of the gospel— God's steady promise of a new life without sin through the work of Jesus Christ. He adhered throughout his life to what he told a fellow friar in 1516:

> Learn Christ and him crucified. Learn to praise him and, despairing of yourself, say, "Lord Jesus, you are my righteousness, just as I am your sin. You have taken upon yourself what is mine and have given to me what I was not." Beware of aspiring to such purity that you will not wish to be looked upon as a sinner, or to be one. For Christ dwells only in sinners. (LW 48:12-13)

This is the spiritual foundation Luther cherished and defended. He did not construct a theological system but shared his chris-

---

18. Roland H. Bainton, *Here I Stand* (New York/Nashville: Abingdon Press, 1950), 298. Quoted also in LW 41:183.

19. Eric W. Gritsch, *Martin—God's Court Jester,* 155-58.

tocentric faith as a spiritual counselor, as a parish pastor, and as a guardian of the enduring truths of the Christian tradition. These truths issued from the spiritual depth of faith in God who was enfleshed in Christ: the authority of scripture; the care for the gospel through a faithful tradition of ministry; the presence of Christ in space and time when the Church communicates him in word and sacrament; good works for the sake of the neighbor in need; life in two realms, one ruled by the word of God, the other by evil in its many ways, yet Christians always on the way to overcome evil; and joyful care for God's good creation with its babies, birds, dogs, and other creatures, reminding Christians to praise God, to be "doxological."

Luther rediscovered and bequeathed to subsequent generations a view of the Church which is always to be reformed: in its teaching tradition, in its structure, and in its moral obligations. For nothing can be unchanging for Christians who are called the people of "the Way" (Acts 9:2), "aliens and exiles" (2 Pt 2:11), "strangers and foreigners on the earth" (Heb 11:13, 14). They constitute a pilgrim Church that "follows constantly the path of penance and renewal."[20]

Luther did not succeed in renewing his Church as much as he thought necessary. But the Church catholic did change because of him; and knowing him better may alert contemporary Christians to the enduring need of renewal for the sake of a faithful mission in the world.[21]

---

20. *Dogmatic Constitution of the Church (Lumen Gentium)* in *Vatican II*, 358:8.

21. Three historical portraits of Luther disclose the breadth and depth of research and interpretation: Martin Brecht, *Martin Luther*, 3 vols., tr. James L. Schaaf (Minneapolis: Fortress Press, 1990-93.); Eric W. Gritsch, *Martin—God's Court Jester. Luther in Retrospect*, 2d. ed. (Ramsey: Sigler Press, 1991); Heiko A. Oberman, *Luther: Man Between God and the Devil*, tr. Eileen Walliser-Schwarzbar (New Haven: Yale University Press, 1989). International Luther Research is listed and evaluated since 1933 in an annual publication entitled *Lutherjahrbuch* (Göttingen: Vandenhoeck & Ruprecht, 1933-).

Abbreviations

BC   *The Book of Concord. The Confessions of the Evangelical Lutheran Church.* Translated and edited by Theodore G. Tappert. Philadelphia: Fortress Press, 1959.

LW   *Luther's Works. American Edition.* 55 vols. Edited by Jaroslav Pelikan and Helmut T. Lehmann. Philadelphia: Fortress Press, 1955-86.

MPL *Patrologia. Series Latina.* 221 vols. Edited by J. P. Migne. Paris, 1844-1904.

WA   *Luthers Werke. Weimar Edition.* Kritische Gesamtausgabe. [Schriften]. Weimar: Boehlau, 1833-.

Acknowledgements

Excerpts from *Luther's Works*, vols. 1-30, used by permission of Concordia Publishing House.

Excerpts from *Luther's Works*, vols. 31, 35, 41, 42, 43, 51, 54, edited by Theodore G. Tappert, Martin O. Dietrich, Gustav K. Wiencke, Theodore Bachmann, Helmut T. Lehman and John Doberstein, Harold Grimm, Eric W. Gritsch, ©1959-69, used by permission of Augsburg Fortress.

Excerpts from *The Book of Concord*, edited by Theodore G. Tappert, ©1959, used by permission of Augsburg Fortress.

Minor stylistic changes (mainly for inclusive language) have been approved by the copyright holders.

The Sense
of
Scripture

The Gospel

Luther's view of the gospel is simply described in *A Brief Instruction on What to Look for and Expect in the Gospels*, 1521. The brief treatise introduces a collection of sermons written at Wartburg Castle, Luther's hideaway from May 1521 until March 1522. The collection became known as the Wartburg Postil ("postil" referring to sermons used in the cycle of the Church year, in this case Advent, Christmas, and Epiphany). In this sermon Luther defines "gospel" as the good news that total faith in Christ creates a new humanity. By completely trusting him, disciples are able to imitate him as an example of love for each other and for others. Such discipleship is the only power to combat the sin of self-love that always tries to make the gospel into a law whose fulfillment is to earn salvation. (Source: LW 35:117-24.)

It is a common practice to number the gospels and to name them by books and say that there are four gospels. . . . There is the still worse practice of regarding the gospels and epistles as law books in which is supposed to be taught what we are to do and in which the works of Christ are pictured to us as nothing but examples. Now where these two erroneous notions remain in the heart, there neither the gospels nor the epistles may be read in a profitable or Christian manner, and [people] remain as pagan as ever.

A Discourse about Christ

One should thus realize that there is only one gospel, but that it is described by many apostles. Every single epistle of Paul and of Peter, as well as the Acts of the Apostles by Luke, is a gospel, even though they do not record all the works and words of Christ, but one is shorter and includes less than another. There is not one of the four major gospels anyway that includes all the words and works of Christ; nor is this necessary. Gospel is and should be nothing else than a discourse or story about Christ, just as happens among people when one writes a book about a king or a prince, telling what he did, said, and suffered in his day. Such a story can be told in various ways; one spins it out, and the other is brief. Thus, the gospel is and should be nothing else than a chronicle, a story, a narrative about Christ, telling who he is, what he did, said, and suffered—a subject which one describes briefly, another more fully, one this way, another that way.

For at its briefest, the gospel is a discourse about Christ, that he is the son of God and became man for us, that he died and was raised, that he has been established as a Lord over all things. This much St. Paul takes in hand and spins out in his epistles. He bypasses all the miracles and incidents [in Christ's ministry] which are set forth in the four gospels, yet he includes the whole gospel adequately and abundantly. This may be seen clearly and well in his greeting to the Romans [1:1-4], where he says what the gospel is and declares, "Paul, a servant of Jesus Christ, called to be an apostle, set apart for the gospel of God which he promised beforehand through his prophets in the holy scriptures, the gospel concerning his Son, who was descended from David according to the flesh and designated Son of God in power according to the Spirit of holiness by his resurrection from the dead, Jesus Christ our Lord," etc.

There you have it. The gospel is a story about Christ, God's and David's Son, who died and was raised and is established as Lord. This is the gospel in a nutshell. Just as there is no more than one Christ, so there is and may be no more than one gospel. Since Paul and Peter too teach nothing but Christ, in the way we have just described, so their epistles can be nothing but the gospel.

Yes, even the teaching of the prophets, in those places where they speak of Christ, is nothing but the true, pure, and proper gospel—just as if Luke or Matthew had described it. For the prophets have proclaimed the gospel and spoke of Christ, as St. Paul here reports and as everyone indeed knows (Rom 1:2). Thus, when Isaiah in chapter 53 says how Christ should die for us and bear our sins, he has written the pure gospel. And I assure you, if we fail to grasp this understanding of the gospel, we will never be able to be illuminated in the scripture nor will we receive the right foundation.

Be sure, moreover, that you do not make Christ into a Moses, as if Christ did nothing more than teach and provide examples as the other saints do; as if the gospel were simply a textbook of teachings or laws. Therefore you should grasp Christ, his words, works, and sufferings, in a twofold manner. First as an example that is presented to you, which you should follow and imitate. As Peter says, "Christ suffered for us, thereby leaving us an example" (1 Pt 2:21). Thus, when you see how he prays, fasts, helps people, and shows them love, so also you should do, both for yourself and for your neighbor. This is however the smallest part of the gospel, on the basis of which it cannot yet even be called gospel. For on this level Christ is of no more help to you than some other saint. His life remains his own and does not as yet contribute anything to you. In short, this mode [of understanding Christ as simply an example] does not make Christians but only hypocrites. You must grasp Christ at a much higher level. Even though this higher level has for a long time been the very best, the preaching of it has been something rare. The chief article and foundation of the gospel is that before you take Christ as an example, you accept and recognize him as a gift, as a present that God has given you and that is your own. This means that when you see or hear of Christ doing or suffering something, you do not doubt that Christ himself, with his deeds and suffering, belongs to you. On this you may depend as surely as if you had done it yourself; indeed as if you were Christ himself. See, this is what it means to have a proper grasp of the gospel, that is, of the overwhelming goodness of God, which neither prophet, nor apostle, nor angel was ever fully able to express, and which no heart could adequately fathom or marvel at. This is the great fire of the love of God for us, whereby the heart and conscience become happy, secure, and content. This is what preaching the Christian faith means. This is why such preaching is called gospel, which in German means a joyful, good, and comforting "message"; and this is why the apostles are called the "twelve messengers."

Gift and Task

Concerning this, Isaiah says, "To us a child is born, to us a son is given" (9:6). If he is given to us, then he must be ours; and so we must also receive him as belonging to us. And Romans says, "How should [God] not give us all things with his Son?" (8:32). See, when you lay hold of Christ as a gift which is given you for your very own and have no doubt about it, you are a Christian. Faith redeems you from sin, death, and hell and enables you to overcome all things. Oh, no one can speak enough about this. It is a pity that this kind of preaching has been silenced in the world, and yet boast is made daily of the gospel.

Now when you have Christ as the foundation and chief blessing of your salvation, then the other part follows: that you take him as your example, giving yourself in service to your neighbor just as you see that Christ has given himself for you. See, there faith and love move forward, God's commandment is fulfilled, and a person is happy and fearless to do and to suffer all things. Therefore make note of this, that Christ as a gift nourishes your faith and makes you a Christian. But Christ as an example exercises your works. These do not make you a Christian. Actually they come forth from you because you have already been made a Christian. As widely as a gift differs from an example, so widely does faith differ from works, for faith possesses nothing of its own, only the deeds and life of Christ. Works have something of your own in them, yet they should not belong to you but to your neighbor.

So you see that the gospel is really not a book of laws and commandments which requires deeds of us, but a book of divine promises in which God promises, offers, and gives us all his possessions and benefits in Christ. The fact that Christ and the apostles provide much good teaching and explain the law is to be counted a benefit just like any other work of Christ. For to teach aright is not the least sort of benefit. We see too that unlike Moses in his book, and contrary to the nature of a commandment, Christ does not horribly force and drive us. Rather he teaches us in a loving and friendly way. He simply tells us what we are to do and what to we are to avoid, what will happen to those who do evil and to those who do good. Christ drives and compels no one. Indeed he teaches so gently that he entices rather than commands. He begins by saying, "Blessed are the poor, blessed are the meek" (Mt 5:3, 5), and so on. And the apostles commonly use the expression, "I admonish, I request, I beseech," and so on. But Moses says, "I command, I forbid," threatening and frightening everyone with horrible punishments and penalties. With this sort of instruction you can now read and hear the gospels profitably.

When you open the book containing the gospels and read or hear how Christ comes here or there, or how someone is brought to him, you should therein perceive the sermon or the gospel through which he is coming to you or you are being brought to him. For the preaching of the gospel is nothing else than Christ coming to us or we being brought to him. When you see how he works, however, and how he helps everyone to whom he comes or who is brought to him, then rest assured that faith is accomplishing this in you and that he is offering your soul exactly the same sort of help and favor through the gospel. If you pause here and let him do you good, that is, if you believe that he benefits and helps you, then you really have it. Then Christ is yours, presented to you as a gift.

After that it is necessary that you turn this into an example and deal with your neighbor in the very same way, be given also to him as a gift and an example. Isaiah speaks of that, "Be comforted, be comforted my dear people, says your Lord God. Say to the heart of Jerusalem, and cry to her, that her sin is forgiven, that her iniquity is ended, that she has received from the hand of God a double kindness for all her sin" (40:1, 2) and so forth. This double kindness is the twofold aspect of Christ:

gift and example. These two are also signified by the double portion of the inheritance which the law of Moses assigns to the eldest son and by many other figures (Dt 21:17).

Rooted in Scripture

What a sin and shame it is that we Christians have come to be so neglectful of the gospel that we not only fail to understand it, but even have to be shown by other books and commentaries what to look for and what to expect in it. The gospels and epistles of the apostles were written for this very purpose. They want themselves to be our guides, to direct us to the writings of the prophets and of Moses in the Old Testament so that we might there read and see for ourselves how Christ is wrapped in swaddling cloths and laid in the manger, that is, how he is comprehended in the writings of the prophets. It is there that people like us should read and study, drill ourselves, and see what Christ is, for what purpose he has been given, how he was promised, and how all scripture tends toward him. For he himself says in John, "If you believed Moses, you would also believe me, for he wrote of me" (5:46). And again, "Search and look up the scriptures, for it is they that bear witness to me" (Jn 5:39).

This is what Paul means in Romans, where in the beginning he says in his greeting, "The gospel was promised by God through the prophets in the holy scriptures" (1:1, 2). This is why the evangelists and apostles always direct us to the scriptures and say, "Thus it is written," and again, "This has taken place in order that the writing of the prophets might be fulfilled," and so forth. In Acts, when the Thessalonians heard the gospel with all eagerness, Luke says that they studied and examined the scriptures day and night in order to see if these things were so (17:11). Thus, when Peter wrote his epistle, right at the beginning he says, "The prophets who prophesied of the grace that was to be yours searched and inquired about this salvation; they inquired what person or time was indicated by the Spirit of Christ within them; and he bore witness through them to the sufferings that were to come upon Christ and the ensuing glory. It was revealed to them that they were serving not themselves but us, in the things which have now been preached among you through the Holy Spirit sent from heaven, things which also the angels long to behold" (1 Pt 1:10-12). What else does Peter here desire than to lead us into the scriptures? It is as if he should be saying, "We preach and open the scriptures to you through the Holy Spirit, so that you yourselves may read and see what is in them and know of the time about which the prophets were writing." For he says as much in Acts: "All the prophets who ever prophesied, from Samuel on, have spoken concerning these days" (3:24).

Therefore, also Luke says in his last chapter that Christ opened the minds of the apostles to understand the scriptures (Lk 24:45). And Christ declares in John that he is the door by which one must enter, and whoever enters by him, to him the gatekeeper (the Holy Spirit) opens in order that he might find pasture and blessedness (Jn 10:9, 3). Thus it is ultimately true that the gospel itself is our guide and instructor in the scriptures. . . .

But what a fine lot of tender and pious children we are! In order that we might not have to study in the scriptures and learn Christ there, we simply regard the entire Old Testament as of no account, as done for and no longer valid. Yet, it alone bears the name of holy scripture. And the gospel should really not be something written, but a spoken word which brought forth the scriptures, as Christ and the apostles have done. This is why Christ himself did not write anything but only spoke. He called his teaching not scripture but gospel, meaning good news or a proclamation that is spread not by pen but by word of mouth. So we go on and make the gospel into a law book, a teaching of commandments, changing Christ into a Moses, changing the One who would help us into a simple instructor. . . .

O would to God that among Christians the pure gospel were known and that most speedily there would be neither use nor need for this work of mine. Then there would surely be hope that the holy scriptures too would come forth again in their worthiness.

Mary's Magnificat

Luther's *Commentary on the Magnificat* of Mary was written during the spring and summer of the year 1521, when Luther was condemned by Church and state. Luther dedicated the commentary to John Frederick, the nephew of Elector Frederick "the Wise." He became a strong supporter of Luther. *The Magnificat* (Lk 1:46-55) shows Luther's reverence for Mary as the model of the Church, an embodiment of unmerited grace. He also recommended Mary's song to politicians who must learn how God uses the lowly in order to humble the proud. (Source: LW 21:299-355.)

In order properly to understand this sacred hymn of praise, we need to bear in mind that the blessed Virgin Mary is speaking on the basis of her own experience, in which she was enlightened and instructed by the Holy Spirit. No one can correctly understand God or his word unless he has received such understanding immediately from the Holy Spirit. But no one can receive it from the Holy Spirit without experiencing, proving, and feeling it. In such experience the Holy Spirit instructs us as in his own school, outside of which nothing is learned but empty words and prattle. When the holy Virgin experienced what great things God was working in her despite her insignificance, lowliness, poverty, and inferiority, the Holy Spirit taught her this deep insight and wisdom, that God is the kind of Lord who does nothing but exalt those of low degree and put down the mighty from their thrones; in short, break what is whole and make whole what is broken.

Just as God in the beginning of creation made the world out of nothing, whence he is called the Creator and the Almighty, so his manner of working continues unchanged. Even now and to the end of the world, all his works are such that out of that which is nothing, worthless, despised, wretched, and dead, he makes that which is something, precious, honorable, blessed, and living. On the other hand, whatever is something, precious, honorable, blessed, and living, he makes to be nothing, worthless, despised, wretched, and dying. No created being can work in this manner; no one can produce anything out of nothing. . . .

Therefore, to God alone belongs that sort of seeing that looks into the depths with their need and misery and is near to all that are lowly. Peter says: "God opposes the proud but gives grace to the humble" (1 Pt 5:5). And this is the source of human love and praise of God. For no one can praise God without first loving him. No one can love him unless God makes himself known to him in the most lovable and intimate fashion. And he can make himself known only through those works of his which he reveals in us, and which we feel and experience within ourselves. But where there is this experience, namely, that he is a God who looks to the lowly and helps only the poor, despised, afflicted, miserable, forsaken, and those who are nothing, there a hearty love for him is born. The heart overflows with gladness and goes leaping and dancing for the great pleasure it has found in God. There the Holy Spirit is present and has taught us in a moment such exceeding great knowledge and gladness through this experience.

For this reason God has also imposed death on us all and laid the cross of Christ, together with countless sufferings and afflictions, on his beloved children and Christians. In fact, sometimes he even lets us fall into sin, in order that he may look to the lowly even more, bring help to many, perform manifold works, show himself a true Creator, and thereby make himself known and worthy of love and praise. . . .

The tender mother of Christ does the same here and teaches us, with her words and by the example of her experience, how to know, love, and praise God. For since she boasts, with heart leaping for joy and praising God, that he regarded her despite her low estate and nothingness, we must believe that she came of poor, despised, and lowly parents. Let us make it very plain for the sake of the simple. Doubtless there were in Jerusalem daughters of the chief priests and counselors who were rich, comely, youthful, cultured, and held in high renown by all the people; even as it is today, with the daughters of kings, princes, and wealthy people. The same was also true of many another city. Even in her own town of Nazareth she was not the daughter of one of the chief rulers, but a poor and plain citizen's daughter, whom none looked up to or esteemed. To her neighbors and their daughters she was but a simple maiden, tending the cattle and doing the housework, and doubtless esteemed no more than any poor maidservant today, who does as she is told around the house. . . .

My soul magnifies God, the Lord . . .

These words express the strong ardor and exuberant joy with which all her mind and life are inwardly exalted in the Spirit. It is as if she said: "My life and all my senses float in the love and praise of God and in lofty pleasures, so that I am no longer mistress of myself; I am exalted, more than I exalt myself, to praise the Lord." This is the experience of all those who are saturated with the divine sweetness and Spirit: They cannot find words to utter what they feel. For to praise the Lord with gladness is not a human work; it is rather a joyful suffering and the work of God alone. It cannot be taught in words but must be learned in one's own experience. . . .

She had no thought but this: If any other maiden had got such good things from God, she would be just as glad and would not grudge them to her; indeed, she regarded herself alone as unworthy of such honor and all others as worthy of it. She would have been well content had God withdrawn these blessings from her and bestowed them upon another before her very eyes. So little did she lay claim to anything but left all of God's gifts freely in his hands, being herself no more than a cheerful guest chamber and willing hostess to so great a guest. Therefore she also kept all these things forever. That is to magnify God alone, to count only him great and lay claim to nothing. We see here how strong an incentive she had to fall into sin, so that it is no less a miracle that she refrained from pride and arrogance than that she received the gifts she did. Tell me, was not hers a wondrous soul? She finds herself the Mother of God, exalted above all mortals, and still remains so simple and so calm that she does not think of any poor serving maid as beneath her. Oh, we poor mortals! If we come into a little wealth or might or honor, or even if we are a little prettier than someone else, we cannot abide being made equal to anyone beneath us, but are puffed up beyond all measure. What should we do if we possessed such great and lofty blessings?

Therefore God lets us remain poor and hapless, because we cannot leave his tender gifts undefiled or keep an even mind, but let our spirits rise or fall according to how he gives or takes away his gifts. But Mary's heart remains the same at all times; she lets God have his will with her and draws from it all only a good comfort, joy, and trust in God. Thus we too should do; that would be to sing a right Magnificat.

. . . and my spirit rejoices in God, my Savior.

We have seen what is meant by "spirit"; it is that which lays hold by faith on things incomprehensible. Mary, therefore, calls God her Savior, or her salvation, even though she neither saw nor felt that this was so, but trusted in sure confidence that he was her Savior and her salvation. This faith came to her through the work God had done within her. And, truly, she sets things in their proper order when she calls God her Lord before calling him her Savior, and when she calls him her Savior before recounting his works. Thereby she teaches us to love and praise God for himself alone, and in the right order, and not selfishly to seek anything at his hands. This is done when one praises God because he is good, regards only his bare goodness, and finds his joy and pleasure in that alone. That is a lofty, pure, and tender mode of loving and praising God and well becomes this Virgin's high and tender spirit.

But the impure and perverted lovers, who are nothing else than parasites and who seek their own advantage in God, neither love nor praise his bare goodness, but have an eye to themselves and consider only how good God is to them, that is, how deeply he makes them feel his goodness and how many good things he does to them. They esteem him highly, are filled with joy, and sing his praises, so long as this feeling continues. But just as soon as he hides his face and withdraws the rays of his goodness, leaving them bare and in misery, their love and praise are at an end. . . .

> *For he has regarded the low estate of his handmaiden. For behold, henceforth all generations will call me blessed.*

The word "low estate" has been translated "humility" by some, as though the Virgin Mary referred to her humility and boasted of it; hence certain prelates also call themselves *humilies*.[1] But that is very wide off the mark, for no one can boast of any good thing in the sight of God without sin and perdition. In his sight we ought to boast only of his pure grace and goodness, which he bestows upon us unworthy ones; so that not our love and praise but his alone may dwell in us and may preserve us. . . .

In scriptural usage, "to humble" means "to bring down" or "to bring to naught." Hence, in the scriptures, Christians are frequently called poor, afflicted, despised. Thus we read in Psalm 116:10: "I am greatly afflicted"—that is, humbled. Humility, therefore, is nothing else than a disregarded, despised, and lowly estate, such as that of persons who are poor, sick, hungry, thirsty, in prison, suffering, and dying. Such was Job in his afflictions, David when he was thrust out of his kingdom, and Christ as well as all Christians, in their distresses. . . .

This, therefore, is what Mary means: "God has regarded me, a poor, despised, and lowly maiden, though he might have found a rich, renowned, noble, and mighty queen, the daughter of princes and great lords. He might have found the daughter of Annas or of Caiaphas, who held the highest position in the land. But he let his pure and gracious eyes light on me and used so poor and despised a maiden, in order that no one might glory in his presence, as though we were worthy of this, and that I

---

1. Apparently Luther is referring to the "Humiliati," a medieval penitential order that arose in the eleventh or twelfth century and was banned in 1571.

must acknowledge it all to be pure grace and goodness and not at all my merit or worthiness. . . ."

Hence she does not glory in her worthiness nor yet in her unworthiness, but solely in the divine regard, which is so exceedingly good and gracious that he deigned to look upon such a lowly maiden, and to look upon her in so glorious and honorable a fashion. They, therefore, do her an injustice who hold that she gloried, not indeed in her virginity, but in her humility. She gloried neither in the one nor in the other, but only in the gracious regard of God. Hence the stress lies not on the words "low estate," but on the word "regarded." For not her humility but God's regard is to be praised. . . .

Thus the words "low estate" show us plainly that the Virgin Mary was a poor, despised, and lowly maiden, who served God in her low estate, not knowing that it was so highly esteemed by him. This should comfort us and teach us that though we should willingly be humbled and despised, we ought not to despair as though God were angry at us. Rather we should set our hope on his grace, concerned only lest we be not cheerful and contented enough in our low estate and lest our evil eye be opened too wide and deceive us by secretly lusting after lofty things and satisfaction with self, which is the death of humility. . . .

Mary begins with herself and sings what he has done for her. Thus she teaches us a twofold lesson. First, every one of us should pay attention to what God does for him rather than to all the works he does for others. For no one will be saved by what God does to another, but only by what he does to you. . . . Remember that God also has his work in you, and base your salvation on no other works than those good works in you alone, as you see the Virgin Mary do here. To let the intercessions of others assist you in this is right and proper; we ought all to pray and work for one another. But no one should depend on the works of others, without the works of God in himself. We should make an effort to regard ourselves and God as though God and we were the only persons in heaven and on earth, and as though God were dealing with no one else than with us. Only then may we also glance at the works of others.

In the second place, she teaches us that we should strive to be foremost in praising God by showing forth the works he has done to us, and then by praising him for the works he has done to others. . . .

Mary confesses that the foremost work God did for her was that he regarded her, which is indeed the greatest of his works, on which all the rest depend and from which they all derive. For where it comes to pass that God turns his face toward one to regard him or her, there is nothing but grace and salvation, and all gifts and works must follow. . . .

Note that she does not say people will speak all manner of good of her, praise her virtues, exalt her virginity or her humility, or sing of what she has done. But for this one thing alone, that God regarded her, people will call her blessed. That is to give all the glory to God as completely as it can be done. Therefore she points to God's regard and says: "For, behold, henceforth all generations will call me blessed. That is, beginning with the time when God regarded my low estate, I shall be called blessed." Not *she* is praised thereby but God's *grace* toward her. . . .

> For he who is mighty has done great things for me,
> and holy is his name.

Here she sings in one breath of all the works that God has done to her and observes the proper order. In the preceding verse she sang of God's regard and gracious good will toward her, which is indeed the greatest and chief work of grace, as we have said. Now she comes to the works and gifts.

Mary does not enumerate any good things in particular but gathers them all together in one word and says, "He has done great things for me." That is: "Everything he has done for me is great." She teaches us here that the greater devotion there is in the heart, the fewer words are uttered. For she feels that however she may strive and try, she cannot express it in words.

Therefore, these few words of the Spirit are so great and profound that no one can comprehend them without having, at least in part, the same Spirit.

The "great things" are nothing less than that she became the Mother of God, in which work so many and such great good things are bestowed on her as pass our understanding. For on this there follows all honor, all blessedness, and her unique place in the whole of humankind, among which she has no equal, namely, that she had a child by the Father in heaven. She herself is unable to find a name for this work, it is too exceedingly great; all she can do is break out in the fervent cry: "They are great things," impossible to describe or define. Hence people have crowded all her glory into a single word, calling her the Mother of God. No one can say anything greater of her or to her, though he had as many tongues as there are leaves on the trees, or grass in the fields, or stars in the sky, or sand by the sea. It needs to be pondered in the heart what it means to be the Mother of God.[2]

"He who is mighty." Truly, in these words she takes away all might and power from every created being and bestows them on God alone. What great boldness and robbery on the part of so young and tender a maiden! She dares, by this one word, to make all the strong feeble, all the mighty weak, all the wise foolish, all the famous despised, and God alone the possessor of all strength, wisdom, and glory.

> *And his mercy is on those who fear him,*
> *from generation to generation.*

Having finished singing about herself and the good things she had from God, and having sung his praises, Mary now

---

2. The title "Mother of God" or, more precisely, "God-Bearer" was officially ascribed to the Virgin Mary at the Council of Ephesus in 431. Throughout his life and theological development, Luther continued to ascribe the title to her, as well as to "call her blessed" in every sense of the word. See Eric W. Gritsch, "The View of Luther and Lutheranism on the Veneration of Mary" in *The One Mediator, the Saints, and Mary: Lutherans and Catholics in Dialogue*, vol. 8, ed. H. George Anderson, J. Francis Stafford, Joseph A. Burgess (Minneapolis: Augsburg, 1992), 379-84.

rehearses all the works of God that he works in general in all people, and sings his praises also for them, teaching us to understand the work, method, nature, and will of God. Many philosophers and persons of great acumen have also engaged in the endeavor to find out the nature of God; they have written much about him, one in this way, another in that, yet all have gone blind over their task and failed of the proper insight. And, indeed, it is the greatest thing in heaven and on earth, to know God correctly if that may be granted to one. This the Mother of God teaches us here in a masterly fashion, if we would only listen, in and by her own experience.

He has helped his servant Israel in remembrance of his mercy. . .

After enumerating the works of God in her and in all people, Mary returns to the beginning and to the chief thing. She concludes the Magnificat by mentioning the very greatest of all God's works—the incarnation of the Son of God. She freely acknowledges herself as the handmaiden and servant of all the world, confessing that this work which was performed in her was not done for her sake alone, but for the sake of all Israel.

*. . . as he spoke to our fathers, to Abraham,
and to his seed forever.*

Here, all merit and presumption are brought low, and God's grace and mercy alone are exalted. For God has not helped Israel on account of their merits, but on account of his own promise. In pure grace he made the promise, in pure grace he also fulfilled it. Wherefore Paul says in Galatians 3:17 that God gave the promise to Abraham four hundred years before he gave the law to Moses, that no one might glory, saying he had merited and obtained such grace and promise through the law or the works of the law. This same promise the Mother of God here lauds and exalts above all else, ascribing this work of the incarnation of God solely to the undeserved promise of divine grace, made to Abraham.

In the first place, it follows from these words of God that

without Christ all the world is in sin and under condemnation and is accursed with all its doing and knowing. For if he says that not some but all nations shall be blessed in Abraham's seed, then without Abraham's seed no nation shall be blessed. . . .

It follows, in the second place, that this seed of Abraham could not be born in the common course of nature, of a man and a woman; for such a birth is cursed [by sin]. . . . Now, if all the world was to be redeemed from the curse by this seed of Abraham and thereby blessed, as the word and oath of God declare, the seed itself had to be blessed first, neither touched nor tainted by that curse, but pure blessing, full of grace and truth (Jn 1:14).

God himself has done this thing. He is able to keep what he has promised, even though no one may understand it before it comes to pass; for his word and work do not demand the proof of reason, but a free and pure faith. Behold how he combined the two. He raises up the seed for Abraham, the natural son of one of his daughters, a pure virgin, Mary, through the Holy Spirit, and without her knowing a man. Here there was no natural conception with its curse [of sin], nor could it touch this seed; and yet it is the natural seed of Abraham, as truly as any of the other children of Abraham. That is the blessed seed of Abraham, in whom all the world is set free from its curse. For whoever believes in this seed, calls upon him, confesses him, and abides in him. . . .

That is what the tender mother of this seed means here by saying: "He has helped his servant Israel, as he promised to Abraham and to all his seed." She found the promise fulfilled in herself; hence she says, "It is now fulfilled; he has brought help and kept his word, solely in remembrance of his mercy." Here we have the foundation of the gospel and see why all its teaching and preaching drive people to faith in Christ and into Abraham's bosom. For where there is not this faith, no other way can be devised and no help given to lay hold of this blessed seed. And indeed, the whole Bible depends on this oath of God, for in the Bible everything has to do with Christ. . . .

When Mary says, "his seed forever," we are to understand "forever" to mean that such grace is to continue Abraham's seed (that is, the Jews) from that time forth, throughout all time, down to the last day.... Let this suffice for the present. We pray God to give us a right understanding of this Magnificat, an understanding that consists not merely in brilliant words but in glowing life in body and soul. May Christ grant us this through the intercession and for the sake of his dear Mother Mary! Amen.

Lectures on Galatians

The letter of Paul to the Galatians was Luther's most favorite description of the word of God as law and gospel. He called the letter his "Katie of Bora," the woman he married in 1525. *The Lectures on Galatians* (1535) began with Luther's summary of "The Argument of St. Paul's Epistle to the Galatians." It is the selected text. In it Luther sees the best biblical summary of dealing with the word of God in distinction from human words. The word of God is "law" by demanding penance; and it is "gospel" by promising forgiveness through Christ alone rather than on the basis of human merit. Human words must show the proper distinction between law and gospel. (Source: LW 26:4-12.)

The Argument of Paul's Epistle to the Galatians

First of all, we must speak of the argument, that is, of the issue with which Paul deals in this epistle. The argument is this: Paul wants to establish the doctrine of faith, grace, the forgiveness of sins or Christian righteousness, so that we may have a perfect knowledge and know the difference between Christian righteousness and all other kinds of righteousness. For righteousness is of many kinds. There is a political righteousness, which the emperor, the princes of the world, philosophers, and lawyers consider. There is also a ceremonial righteousness, which human traditions teach, as, for example, the traditions of the pope and other traditions. Parents and teachers may teach this righteousness without danger, because they do not attribute to it any power to make satisfaction for sin, to placate God, and to earn grace; but they teach that these ceremonies are necessary only for moral discipline and for certain observances. There is, in addition to these, yet another righteousness, the righteousness of the law or of the Decalogue, which Moses teaches. We too teach this, but after the doctrine of faith.

Christian Righteousness

Over and above all these there is the righteousness of faith or Christian righteousness, which is to be distinguished most carefully from all the others. . . . Also the righteousness of works is a gift of God, as are all the things we have. But this most excellent righteousness, the righteousness of faith, which God imputes to us through Christ without works, is neither political nor ceremonial nor legal nor work-righteousness, while all the others . . . are active. For here we work nothing, render nothing to God; we only receive and permit someone else to work in us, namely, God. Therefore it is appropriate to call the righteousness of faith or Christian righteousness "passive." This is a righteousness hidden in a mystery, which the world does not understand. In fact, Christians themselves do not adequately understand it or grasp it in the midst of their temptations. Therefore it must always be taught and continually exercised. And anyone who does not grasp or take hold of it in afflictions and terrors of conscience cannot stand. For there is no comfort of conscience so solid and certain as is this passive righteousness.

But such is human weakness and misery that in the terrors of conscience and in the danger of death we look at nothing except our own works, our worthiness, and the law. When the law shows us our sin, our past life immediately comes to our mind. Then the sinner groans in his great anguish of mind and says: "Oh, how damnably I have lived! If only I could live longer! Then I would amend my life." Thus, human reason cannot refrain from looking at active righteousness, that is, its own righteousness; nor can it shift its gaze to passive, that is, Christian righteousness, but it simply rests in the active righteousness. So deeply is this evil rooted in us, and so completely have we acquired this unhappy habit! Taking advantage of the weakness of our nature, Satan increases and aggravates these thoughts in us. Then it is impossible for the conscience to avoid being more seriously troubled, confounded, and frightened. For it is impossible for the human mind to conceive any comfort of itself, or to look only at grace amid its consciousness and terror of sin, or consistently to reject all discussion of works. To do this is beyond human power and thought. Indeed, it is even beyond the law of God. For although the law is the best of all things in the world, it still cannot bring peace to a terrified conscience but makes it even sadder and drives it to despair. For by the law sin becomes exceedingly sinful (Rom 7:13).

Therefore the afflicted conscience has no remedy against despair and eternal death except to take hold of the promise of grace offered in Christ, that is, this righteousness of faith, this passive or Christian righteousness, which says with confidence: "I do not seek active righteousness. I ought to have and perform it; but I declare that even if I did have it and perform it, I cannot trust in it or stand up before the judgment of God on the basis of it. Thus I put myself beyond all active righteousness, all righteousness of my own or of the divine law, and I embrace only that passive righteousness, which is the righteousness of grace, mercy, and the forgiveness of sins." In other words, this is the righteousness of Christ and of the Holy Spirit, which we do not perform but receive, which we do not have but accept, when God the Father grants it to us through Jesus Christ.

As the earth itself does not produce rain and is unable to acquire it by its own strength, worship, and power but receives it only by a heavenly gift from above, so this heavenly righteousness is given to us by God without our work or merit. As much as the dry earth of itself is able to accomplish in obtaining the right and blessed rain, that much can we accomplish by our own strength and works to obtain that divine, heavenly, and eternal righteousness. Thus we can obtain it only through the free imputation and indescribable gift of God. Therefore, the highest art and wisdom of Christians is not to know the law, to ignore works and all active righteousness, just as outside the people of God the highest wisdom is to know and study the law, works, and active righteousness.

Two Realms

It is a marvelous thing and unknown to the world to teach Christians to ignore the law and to live before God as though there were no law whatever. For if you do not ignore the law and thus direct your thoughts to grace, as though there were no law but as though there were nothing but grace, you cannot be saved. "For through the law comes knowledge of sin" (Rom 3:20). On the other hand, works and the performance of the law must be demanded in the world as though there were no promise or grace. This is because of the stubborn, proud, and hardhearted, before whose eyes nothing must be set except the law, in order that they may be terrified and humbled. For the law was given to terrify and kill the stubborn and to exercise the old self. Both words must be correctly divided, according to the apostle (2 Tm 2:25ff.).

This calls for a wise and faithful father who can moderate the law in such a way that it stays within its limits. For if I were to teach the law in such a way that we suppose ourselves to be justified by it before God, I would be going beyond the limit of the law, confusing these two righteousnesses, the active and the passive, and would be a bad dialectician who does not properly distinguish. But the flesh or the old self, the law and works, are all joined together. In the same way the spirit or the new self is joined to the promise and to grace. Therefore, when I see that persons are sufficiently contrite, oppressed by the law, terrified by sin, and thirsting for comfort, then it is time for me to take the law and active righteousness from their sight and to set forth before them, through the gospel, the passive righteousness which excludes Moses and the law and shows the promise of Christ, who came for the afflicted and for sinners. Here they are raised up again and gain hope. Nor are they any longer under the law; they are under grace, as the apostle says: "The law, until Christ" (Rom 6:14). When he came, Moses and the law stopped. So did circumcision, sacrifices, and the Sabbath. So did all the prophets.

Proper Distinctions

This is our theology, by which we teach a precise distinction between these two kinds of righteousness, the active and the passive, so that morality and faith, works and grace, secular society and religion may not be confused. Both are necessary, but both must be kept within their limits. Christian righteousness applies to the new self, and the righteousness of the law applies to the old self, who is born of flesh and blood. Upon this latter, as upon an ass, a burden must be put that will oppress it. It must not enjoy the freedom of the spirit or of grace unless it has first put on the new self by faith in Christ, but this does not happen fully in this life. Then it may enjoy the kingdom and the ineffable gift of grace. . . .

We set forth two worlds, as it were, one of them heavenly and the other earthly. Into these we place these two kinds of righteousness, which are distinct and separated from each other. The righteousness of the law is earthly and deals with earthly things; by it we perform good works. But as the earth does not bring forth fruit unless it has first been watered and made fruitful from above—for the earth cannot judge, renew, and rule the heavens, but the heavens judge, renew, rule, and fructify the earth, so that it may do what the Lord has commanded—so also by the righteousness of the law we do nothing even when we do much; we do not fulfill the law even when we fulfill it. . . .

Then do we do nothing and work nothing in order to obtain this righteousness? I reply: Nothing at all. For this righteousness means to do nothing, to hear nothing, and to know nothing about the law or about works but to know and believe only this: that Christ has gone to the Father and is now invisible; that he sits in heaven at the right hand of the Father, not as a judge but as one who has been made for us wisdom, righteousness, sanctification, and redemption from God (1 Cor 1:30); in short, that he is our High Priest, interceding for us and reigning over us and in us through grace. Here one notices no sin and feels no terror or remorse of conscience. Sin cannot happen in this Christian righteousness; for where there is no law, there cannot be any transgression (Rom 4:15). If, therefore, sin does not have a place here, there is no conscience, no terror, no sadness. Therefore John says: "No one born of God commits sin" (1 Jn 3:9). But if there is any conscience or fear present, this is a sign that this righteousness has been withdrawn, that grace has been lost sight of, and that Christ is hidden and out of sight. But where Christ is truly seen, there must be full and perfect joy in the Lord and peace of heart. There the heart declares: "Although I am a sinner according to the law, judged by the righteousness of the law, nevertheless I do not despair. I do not die, because Christ lives who is my righteousness and my eternal and heavenly life. In that righteousness and life I have no sin, conscience, and death. I am indeed a sinner according to the present life and its righteousness, as a son of Adam where the law accuses me, death reigns and devours me. But above this life I have another righteousness, another life, which is Christ, the Son of God, who does not know sin and death but is righteousness and eternal life. For his sake this body of mine will be raised from the dead and delivered from the slavery of the law and sin, and will be sanctified together with the spirit."

Thus as long as we live here, both remain. The flesh is accused, exercised, saddened, and crushed by the active righteousness of the law. But the spirit rules, rejoices, and is saved by passive righteousness, because it knows that it has a Lord sitting in heaven at the right hand of the Father. He has abolished the law, sin, and death, and has trodden all evils underfoot, has led them captive and triumphed over them in himself (Col 2:15). In this epistle, therefore, Paul is concerned to instruct, comfort, and sustain us diligently in a perfect knowledge of this most excellent and Christian righteousness. For if the doctrine of justification is lost, the whole of Christian doctrine is lost. . . . This distinction is easy to speak of; but in experience and practice it is the most difficult of all, even if you exercise and practice it diligently. For in the hour of death or in other conflicts of conscience these two kinds of righteousness come together more closely than you would wish or ask.

Therefore I admonish you, especially those of you who are to become instructors of consciences, as well as each of you individually, that you exercise yourselves by study, by reading, by meditation, and by prayer, so that in temptation you will be able to instruct consciences, both your own and others, console them, and take them from the law to grace, from active righteousness to passive righteousness, in short, from Moses to Christ. In affliction and in the conflict of conscience it is the devil's habit to frighten us with the law and to set against us the consciousness[1] of sin, our wicked past, the wrath and judgment of God, hell, and eternal death, so that thus he may drive us into despair, subject us to himself, and pluck us from Christ. It is also his habit to set against us those passages in the gospel in which Christ himself requires works from us, and with plain words threatens damnation to those who do not perform them. If here we cannot distinguish between these two kinds of righteousness, if here by faith we do not take hold of Christ, who is sitting at the right hand of God, who is our life and our righteousness, and who makes intercession for us miserable sinners before the Father (Heb 7:25), then we are under the law and not under grace, and Christ is no longer a savior. Then he is a lawgiver. Then there can be no salvation left, but sure despair and eternal death will follow.

Therefore let us learn diligently this art of distinguishing between these two kinds of righteousness, in order that we may know how far we should obey the law. . . . When I have this righteousness within me, I descend from heaven like the rain that makes the earth fertile. That is, I come forth into another kingdom, and I perform good works whenever the opportunity arises. If I am a minister of the word, I preach, I comfort the saddened, I administer the sacraments. If I am a father, I rule my household and family, I train my children in piety and honesty. If I am a magistrate, I perform the office which I have received by divine

---

1. Here, as in some other passages in Luther's writings, the Latin word *conscientia* has the meaning "consciousness" rather than the more specific meaning "conscience."

command. If I am a servant, I faithfully tend to my master's affairs. In short, those who know for sure that Christ is their righteousness, not only cheerfully and gladly work in their calling, but also submit themselves for the sake of love to magistrates and their laws, and to everything else in this present life—even, if need be, to burden and danger. For they know that God wants this and that this obedience pleases him.

So far the argument of the epistle, which Paul sets forth because of the false teachers who had obscured this righteousness of faith among the Galatians. Against them he asserts his authority and office.

Noah and the Flood

This selection from Luther's commentary on the Book of Genesis shows how Luther identified with the biblical story of humankind. He understood himself to be part of that story as a member of the Christian Church rooted in the divine history of salvation. He devoted thirty-two years of his teaching career to the study of the Bible, mainly the Old Testament. That is why he would be called to a position of being Professor of Old Testament today.[1] He spent only three or four years on the study of the New Testament. Luther was particularly drawn to the figure of Noah because he saw his own life in the portrayal of Noah's survival through divine intervention. The selection is from Luther's massive commentary on Genesis 6:5–9:16. (Source: LW 2:44-171.)

The Hidden God

It is in this manner that God saw human wickedness and repented. That is, Noah, who had the Holy Spirit and was a minister of the word, saw the wickedness of humanity and through the Holy Spirit was moved to grief when he observed this situation. Paul also similarly declares that the Holy Spirit is grieved in the godly by the ungodliness and wickedness of the ungodly (Eph 4:30). Because Noah is a faithful minister of the word and the mouthpiece of the Holy Spirit, Moses correctly states that the Holy Spirit is grieving when Noah grieves and wishes that humanity would rather not be in existence than be so evil.

Therefore, the meaning is not that God from eternity had not seen these conditions; he sees everything from eternity. But since this wickedness now manifests itself with the utmost violence, God now discloses it in the hearts of his ministers and prophets.

---

1. This is the view of the German Luther scholar Heinrich Bornkamm, *Luther and the Old Testament* (tr. Eric W. And Ruth C. Gritsch; ed. Victor I. Gruhn, Philadelphia: Fortress, 1969), 7.

Thus God is immutable and unchanging in his counsel from eternity. He sees and knows all things; but he does not reveal them to the godly except at his own fixed time, so that they themselves may see them too. This seems to me to be the simplest meaning of this passage, and Augustine's interpretation differs little from it.

I follow this general rule: to avoid as much as possible any questions that carry us to the throne of the supreme Majesty. It is better and safer to stay at the manger of Christ the man. For there is very great danger in involving oneself in the mazes of the divine Being.

To this passage belong others that are similar; in them God is depicted as though he had eyes, ears, a mouth, a nose, hands, and feet. This is the way Isaiah, Daniel, and the other prophets saw him in their visions. In such passages scripture speaks about God no differently from the way it speaks about a human being. . . .

It is for this reason that God lowers himself to the level of our weak comprehension and presents himself to us in images, in coverings, as it were, in simplicity adapted to a child, that in some measure it may be possible for him to be known by us. Thus the Holy Spirit appeared in the form of a dove, not because he is a dove (Mt 3:16). Yet in that simple form he wanted to be known, received, and worshiped; for he was truly the Holy Spirit. Likewise, in the same passages, even though no one will maintain that God the Father was the voice sounding from heaven, he nevertheless had to be received and worshiped in this simple image. . . .

We maintain that Noah's heart was moved by the Holy Spirit, so that he realized that God was angry with humanity and wanted to destroy it. Moreover, this is an understandable interpretation, one that does not involve us in discussions about the absolute power or majesty of God, which are fraught with very great dangers, as I have seen in the instance of many people. Such spirits are first puffed up by the devil to believe that they have the Holy Spirit; they disregard the word; yes, they even blaspheme, and they boast of nothing but the Spirit and visions.

This is the first stage of error, when people disregard God as he has enveloped himself and become incarnate, and seek to scrutinize the unveiled God. Later on, when the hour of judgment arrives and they feel the wrath of God, when God is judging and investigating their hearts, then the devil ceases to puff them up, and they despair and die. For they are walking unsheltered in the sun and are abandoning the shade which gives relief from the heat (Is 4:6).

Let no one, therefore, contemplate the unveiled divinity, but let them flee from these contemplations as from hell and the veritable temptations of Satan. Let it be the concern of each of us to abide by the signs by which God has revealed himself to us, namely, his Son, born of the Virgin Mary and lying in his manger among the cattle; the word; baptism; the Lord's Supper; and absolution. In these images we see and meet a God whom we can bear, one who comforts us, lifts us up into hope, and saves us. . . .

The incarnate Son of God is, therefore, the covering in which the divine Majesty presents himself to us with all his gifts, and does so in such a manner that there is no sinner too wretched to be able to approach him with the firm assurance of obtaining pardon. This is the one and only view of the divinity that is available and possible in this life. But on the last day those who have died in this faith will be so enlightened by heavenly power that they will see even the divine Majesty itself. Meanwhile we must come to the Father by that way which is Christ himself; he will lead us safely, and we shall not be deceived. . . .

The very holy man Noah, together with his father and his grandfather, wastes away with grief when he sees the dreadful wrath of God. Noah takes no pleasure in the ruin of the entire human race but is worried and greatly troubled. Meanwhile people are living in the utmost smugness. They laugh and rejoice; they even scoff at him. Psalm 109:4 describes a similar situation: "In return for my love they accuse me, even as I make prayer for them." Paul says in Philippians 3:18: "I tell you with tears." What else can holy people do when the world absolutely refuses to mend its ways?

This is the perpetual characteristic of the true Church: It not only experiences suffering and is dishonored and held in contempt, but it also prays for those who afflict it and is gravely concerned about their perils. In contrast, the closer the ungodly are to their condemnation, the greater is the smugness with which they indulge in amusements and pleasures. Therefore, when the hour of judgment arrives, God, on the other hand, closes his ears to such an extent that he does not even hear his beloved children as they pray and beg for mercy for the ungodly. Ezekiel complains that no one is found to set himself up as a wall in Israel's behalf, a function that properly belongs to the prophets, according to him (13:5). . . .

It is an awful example that God did not spare the first world when Noah, Lamech, and Methuselah set themselves up like a wall. What shall we suppose will happen when there are no such walls, that is, when there is no Church at all? The Church is always a wall against the wrath of God. It grieves, it agonizes, it prays, it pleads, it teaches, it preaches, it admonishes, as long as the hour of judgment has not yet arrived but is impending. When it sees that these activities are of no avail, what else can it do than grieve deeply over the destruction of impenitent people? Seeing a large number of their kinsmen and relatives about to perish increased the grief of the godly fathers.

This grief Moses was unable to portray in a better and clearer manner than to state that the Lord was sorry that he had made the human being. When he describes the human nature, which was fashioned according to the image of God, he states that God saw everything that he had made, and that it was very good (Gn 1:31). Thus the Lord delights and rejoices in his created beings. In this passage he changes his opinion completely and states the opposite, namely, that he grieves and is sorry that he ever made the human being. . . .

The careful consideration of all this is profitable to fortify us against being offended by the smugness of the ungodly. For the same things that happened to Noah happen to us. . . .

Therefore we lament with Noah and commit our cause to the

Lord, just as Christ did on the cross; for what else are we to do? We wait for God to sit in judgment on the earth and to make it clear that he loves the remnant of those who fear him and hates the Mass of the unrepentant sinners, even though they boast that they are the Church, that they have the promises, and that they have the worship of God. Thus he destroyed the entire original world and made his promise concerning the seed come true for that wretched and tiny remnant, Noah and his sons. . . .

Such great wrath of the divine Majesty would have slain him if God had not added the promise to preserve him. Nevertheless, it is likely that his faith was still troubled even though he heard this promise. It is unbelievable how much the contemplation of the wrath of God depresses the heart.

Furthermore, here there is a new expression of the Holy Spirit—an expression which the heavenly messenger Gabriel also employs when addressing the Blessed Virgin: "You have found favor with God" (Lk 1:30). This expression very clearly rules out any merit and gives praise to faith, by which alone we are justified before God, that is, are acceptable to God and please him. . . .

When all these people became corrupt, Noah alone remained steadfast, a truly amazing man. He turned aside neither to the left nor to the right; he retained the true worship of God; he kept the pure doctrine and lived in the fear of God. There is, therefore, no doubt that the perverse generation hated him intensely and harassed him in various ways while exposing him to ridicule: "Is it you alone who is wise? Is it you alone who pleases God? Are all the rest of us in error? Shall we all be condemned? Is it you alone who is not in error? Is it you alone who will not be condemned?" Therefore the righteous and holy man had to determine by himself that all the others were in error and should be condemned, but that only he, together with his descendants, would be saved. Even though he reached this correct conclusion, it was very difficult. Thus the holy man wrestled with various thoughts like these. . . .

He is declared righteous through his faith in God, because he believed first the universal promise about the seed of the woman and later on also the special one about the destruction of the world by the flood and about the preservation of his descendants. He is declared perfect because he walked in the fear of God and carefully avoided murder and the other sins with which the ungodly were polluting themselves in violation of their conscience; and he was no way influenced by the many offenses of the most distinguished, the wisest, and, in appearance, the holiest people.

This was an outstanding virtue. To us today it seems impossible that one man should defy the entire world and condemn as evil all the rest, who glory in the Church, the word, and the worship of God, and that he should maintain that he alone is a son of God and acceptable to God. Noah, accordingly, is truly an amazing man. . . .

Just as before the flood a new Church begins in paradise through Adam and Eve, who believed the promise, so at this point also a new world and a new Church take their beginning from Noah's marriage; it is the seedbed, as it were, of that world which is to endure until the end of the world. . . .

Punishment

After Noah and his people had cried for a long time and had blamed the wickedness of the world, the Lord finally indicated that he, too, saw the wickedness and intended to punish it. This second stage we are waiting for today; and there is no doubt that there will be some to whom the coming destruction of the world will be revealed, unless perhaps that destruction will be the last day and the last judgment. . . .

Reason cannot believe there can be such wrath. Nor can reason understand it adequately. See how different these words are from the former! We heard that God saw everything he had made, and it was very good (Gn 1:31). He also bestowed upon man and beast the blessing of increase. He placed the earth and all the riches of the earth under human rule (Gn 1:28). He

added—and this is most important—the promise concerning
the seed of the woman and of eternal life. He estalished not only
the household and the state but also the Church (Gn 3:15). How,
then, does it happen that the first world, which, as Peter ex-
presses it, was established by the word in this manner, perishes
by water (2 Pt 3:5-6)? . . .

What is the reason for this great wrath? Certainly, as the text
states here, it is to be found in the fact that the earth is filled with
violence. An amazing reason! The text says nothing about the
First Table [the first three commandments of the Decalogue]; it
stresses only the Second Table [the fourth to the tenth commandment of the Decalogue], as though God intended to say:
"About myself I shall say nothing. I shall not say that they hate,
blaspheme, and persecute my name and word. How disgracefully they live among themselves! Neither the household nor
the state is properly managed; everything is done with violence,
nothing with reason and law. Therefore I shall destroy both
humanity and the earth. . . ."

There were two results of the flood: Human power was
diminished; and human wealth, together with that of the earth,
was reduced. The fruits that the trees produced were utterly
unlike those they bore before the flood. Before the flood turnips
were better than melons, oranges, or pomegranates were after-
wards. Pears were more delicious than spices are today. The
strength in a man's finger was probably greater than it is today
in his entire arm. In like manner, his reason and wisdom were
far superior. But God inflicted punishment because of sin not
only on humanity but also on its possessions and dominion, in
order that his wrath might also be a lesson for his descendants.

How does he bring about the destruction? It is obvious that
he takes the element water and destroys everything. The force
with which this element is wont to rage is well known. Even
though the air may be pestilential, it does not always contami-
nate trees and roots. But water not only demolishes everything
and not only tears out trees and roots, but it carries away the
very surface of the earth and alters the soil, so that even the most

fertile fields are ruined by the saltiness of the earth and by the sand. This was the destruction of the first world. . . .

Ark and Flood

Someone may ask: Why does God give such detailed directions about everything? The command about getting the ark ready was enough. So far as space and the method of construction are concerned, reason itself sees what must be done, as many outstanding works of craftsmen prove. Why, then, does God instruct Noah so carefully about the length, the width, and the height of the ark, and about covering it with bitumen? Surely in order that Noah, after preparing everything in accordance with God's direction (just as Moses patterned the tabernacle after the original on the mountain), might believe with greater confidence that he and his people would be preserved, and that he might not become distrustful of the task that God himself had assigned and had given him orders how to perform. This is the reason why God gives such careful directions about everything. . . .

How terrible a situation it is that of the entire human race only eight persons are chosen to be saved and that even among these, Ham, Noah's third son, is eventually rejected! By God's own mouth he is actually listed among the chosen and holy; yes, he is even protected and saved with them, and no distinction can be made between him and his father Noah. If he had not had the same beliefs and had not prayed, if he had not feared God, he would in no wise have been saved in the ark; and yet later on he is rejected. . . .

Someone may ask: What, then, shall we conclude from these occurrences? Nothing else than that they are presented to us to produce in us the fear of God, so that we do not assume that we cannot fall from grace after we have once received grace. Paul likewise issued the warning: "Let anyone who thinks that he stands take heed lest he fall" (1 Cor 10:12). Therefore these occurrences should serve to keep us humble, so that we do not become proud about our gifts or slothfully come to a standstill with what we have received but rather press on to what lies ahead, as Paul says in Philippians 3:13, and not assume that we have fully obtained everything. . . .

Noah is praised as an example for us because he did not have a dead faith, which is actually no faith at all, but a living and active faith. He is obedient when God gives him a command; and because he believes God both when he gives a promise and when he utters a threat, he painstakingly carries out God's direction in regard to the ark, the gathering of the animals, and the food.

The particular praise of Noah's faith is that he stays on the royal road; he adds nothing, changes nothing, and takes nothing away from God's directive but abides completely by the command he hears. . . .

We should consider, not what is commanded, but who gives the command. Who does not do this will often take offense at either the triviality or the senselessness, if I may express myself in this manner, of the task. But we must give God praise for wisdom and goodness, and maintain that whatever he himself commands is commanded with the utmost wisdom and goodness, even though reason judges otherwise. . . .

It was no joke or laughing matter for them to live shut up in the ark for so long, to see the endless masses of rain, to be tossed about by the waves, and to drift. In these circumstances there was the feeling that God had forgotten them, as Moses indicates when he states that the Lord at last remembered Noah and his sons. Even though they overcame this feeling through faith, they did not overcome it without great annoyance to the flesh. Similarly, a young man who leads a chaste life indeed overcomes lust, yet certainly not without the greatest discomfort and effort. But in this instance the danger was greater, for all their circumstances compelled them to debate whether God was favorably inclined and wanted to remember them. Therefore, although they overcame these hardships, they did not overcome them without awful affliction. There is nothing that the flesh, which is inherently weak, is less able to tolerate than a God who does not remember us but has forgotten us. If by nature we are so constituted that we become puffed up and haughty when God remembers us, grants us success, and is favorable toward us, what is so remarkable about our becoming disheartened and despondent when God seems to have cast us aside and everything goes wrong?

Let us, then, remember that this story sets before us an example of faith, perseverance, and patience, in order that those who have the divine promise may not only learn to believe it but may also realize that they need perseverance. But perseverance does not come without a great struggle. In the New Testament Christ calls on us to persevere when he says: "He who endures to the end will be saved" (Mt 24:13). . . .

So far, by his work, God has shown that he has been appeased and, as it were, has been changed from an angry God to a merciful one, since he restrains the waters and dries up the earth. Now he continues to strengthen this comfort with his word. He addresses Noah in a friendly manner and commands him, together with the rest of the human beings and the animals, to leave the ark. . . .

Noah could have thought thus: "Behold, at the command of the Lord I constructed the ark, and I was saved in it when all humanity was perishing. Therefore I shall remain in it, or I shall keep it as a temple or a place for the worship of God; for it has been hallowed by the word of God and by the fact that saints, or the Church, dwell in it." But the godly man does nothing of the kind, because the word commanded him to leave. Therefore he complies; and now that the ark has served its purpose during the time of the flood, he abandons it and is convinced that he and his children must live on the earth.

Likewise, let us institute nothing without the word of God; but let us walk in a holy calling, that is, in one that has the word and command of God. Who institutes anything without the command of God labors in vain. . . .

Therefore, let us remember not to institute anything without the command of God. Because duties are different, the works of individuals can not and need not be the same. How absurd it would be for me to shout that I must follow the example of the emperor and that I must dictate laws to others! How wicked it would be if I maintained that I must follow the example of the judge, and condemned someone to execution by the gallows or by the sword! Attention must, therefore, be directed, not to the works of an individual but to his or her faith. One faith is common to all the saints, although their works differ very much. . . .

Blessed to Be Fruitful and in Command

Noah realized that God is indeed favorably inclined toward him; for he is not satisfied with that first blessing with which he blessed the human race at the creation of the world, but he adds this new one in order that Noah may have no doubt whatever concerning the future increase of his progeny. This promise was all the more welcome because God had previously given the express promise that he would never again rage against the human race with so severe a punishment.

For one thing, this confirms marriage; for through his word and command God joins the male with the female, and that for the definite purpose of filling the earth with human beings. Because before the flood God had been provoked to wrath by the sin of lust, it was necessary, on account of this awful expression of wrath, to show now that God does not hate or condemn the lawful union of a man and a woman but wants the human race to be propagated by it.

This was a sure proof for Noah that God actually loves man and woman, is well disposed toward them, and has now put away all wrath. He wants human beings to be propagated through the union of a man and a woman. . . .

This blessing, which gives this authority over the beasts to man, must not be taken lightly. It is an extraordinary gift, of which the heathen, who are without the word, have no knowledge. And we enjoy the benefit of this gift most. When these words were addressed to Noah and this privilege was granted to him, there was no need for it. A small number of human beings occupied the entire earth; so there was a superabundance of the fruits of the earth, and it was unnecessary to add the flesh of the beasts. But today we could not live on the fruits of the earth alone if this great gift had not been added, which permits us to eat the flesh of beasts, birds, and fish.

These words, therefore, establish the butcher shop; attach hares, chickens, and geese to the spit; and fill the tables with all sorts of foods. Necessity also keeps people busy. Not only do they hunt forest animals, but at home they give particular care to tending and fattening cattle for food.

In this passage God sets himself up as a butcher; for with his word he slaughters and kills the animals that are suited for food, in order to make up, as it were, for the great sorrow that pious Noah experienced during the flood. For this reason God thinks Noah ought to be provided for more sumptuously now.

We must not assume that these things happen by chance, as do the heathen, who are of the opinion that the custom of butchering animals always existed. These things are established, or rather permitted, by the word of God. An animal could not have been slain without sin unless God by his word had clearly given permission to do so. It is a great liberty that with impunity man may kill and eat animals of every edible kind. If only one kind of animal had been designated for this purpose, it would still be a great blessing. How much greater a blessing it must be considered that all animals fit for food are permitted! . . .

After God has permitted the killing of cattle, not only for sacrifices but also for food, and has forbidden homicide, there now follows the reason why he detests homicide so intensely: He wants the human race to multiply on the earth; but homicides lay waste the earth and bring on desolation, just as we observe in war. God did not create the earth without a purpose; he wanted it to be inhabited, as Isaiah says (45:18). For this reason he also makes it fruitful by means of rain and sunshine. Hence he hates those who remove from the earth those who inhabit it. For his will is life, not death (Ps 30:5). . . .

The Rainbow

This sign should remind us to give thanks to God. For as often as the rainbow appears, it preaches to the entire world with a loud voice about the wrath which once moved God to destroy the whole world. It also gives comfort, that we may have the conviction that God is kindly inclined toward us again and will never again make use of so horrible a punishment. Thus it teaches the fear of God and faith at the same time, the greatest virtues. . . .

I hold that the rainbow was a new creature, not seen by the world until now, in order that the world might be reminded of the past wrath, of which the rainbow shows traces, and might also be assured of the mercy of God. It is like a book or a picture that shows both the bygone wrath and the present grace.

There is also a discussion about the colors, which some consider to be four: fiery, yellow, green, and watery or blue. But I myself think there are only two, a fiery one and a watery one. Moreover, the fiery one is uppermost, except when the rainbow is reflected; for then, just as in a mirror, the uppermost parts are changed to the lowest. When the fiery and the watery color come together or are mixed, the result is a yellow color.

The nature of the colors was so decreed by God with the definite purpose, not only that the watery color might be a reminder of the bygone wrath, but also that the fiery one might depict the future judgment for us. The inner surface, which has the color of water, is finite; but the outside, which has the color of fire, is infinite. Thus the first world perished by the flood, but the wrath had limits. For some remnants were saved; and afterward another world came into being, yet one that was finite. But when God destroys the world with fire, this physical life will not be restored; but the wicked will bear the eternal

judgment of death in fire, while the godly will be raised into a
new and everlasting life—not a physical one, even though it is
in bodies, but a spiritual one. . . .

Conclusion

God should be praised and blessed forever for dealing with
his saints in a truly wonderful manner. For while he permits
them to be weak and to stumble, while he lets them abound with
actions that result in displeasure and offense, and the world
judges and condemns them, he forgives them these weaknesses
and has compassion on them. On the other hand, he leaves to
Satan and utterly rejects those who are angels in their own eyes.

The first value of this account is that the godly have the
comfort they need in their weaknesses, because they see that at
times even the saintliest persons fell disgracefully as the result
of a similar weakness.

In the second place, the account is also an example of the
terrible judgment of God. Prompted by Ham's peril, we should
not at once pass judgment if we see a person who holds an
official position in the state or the Church or the home—such as
our parents—make a mistake and fall. For who knows why God
is doing this? Even though such lapses should not be excused,
we see that they are profitable to comfort the godly; for they
show that God is able to put up with the mistakes and faults of
his people. When we are assailed by sins, therefore, we too may
hope for God's mercy and not despair.

But this medicine for the godly is poison for the ungodly.
They are not looking for instruction and comfort from God.
Therefore they do not deserve to see the glory of God in his
saints. They see nothing except what offends and ensnares them
so that they fall, and in the end they themselves perish. . . .

Hence when we see saints fall, let us not be offended. Much
less let us gloat over the weakness of other people, or rejoice, as
though we were stronger, wiser, and holier. Rather, let us bear
with and cover, and even extenuate and excuse, such mistakes

as much as we can, bearing in mind that what the other person has experienced today we may perhaps experience tomorrow. We are all one mass, and we are all born of one flesh. Therefore let us learn Paul's rule that "he who stands should take heed lest he fall" (1 Cor 10:12).

This is the way Ham's brothers looked upon their drunken parents. They thought: "Behold, our father has fallen. But God deals in a wonderful way with his saints. Sometimes he lets them fall for our comfort, lest we despair when we are overcome by a similar weakness."

Let us too emulate this wisdom. The sins of other people do not give us the power to judge them. "They stand and fall for their own lord" (Rom 14:4). Furthermore, if the downfall of others displeases us—let us be on our guard all the more diligently, lest something of the same sort happen to us; but let us not judge proudly and presumptuously. For this is the vicious character of original sin, that it wants to be wise beyond measure and seeks to acquire praise for righteousness as the result of other people's failing.

We are indeed weak sinners, and we readily confess that since we are human our behavior is not always free of offense. But although we have this fault in common with our opponents, we diligently do our duty by planting the word of God, teaching the Churches, correcting defects, exhorting to what is right, comforting the weak, and whatever else is called for by the ministry that God has committed to us.

The Sum of the Christian Life

In a sermon of 1532 Luther used 1 Timothy 1:5-7 as the biblical foundation to sum up his view of the Christian life. The Timothy text admonishes Paul's young coworker to instruct people in such a way that they become filled with love "that comes from a pure heart, a good conscience, and sincere faith." Luther preached the sermon to a mixed audience of princes and common folk. (Source: LW 51:260-87.)

Dear friends, you know how earnestly God has commanded everyone to hear and to learn his precious word, for it cost him much to bring it to the world. He hazarded his prophets for this purpose, indeed, he even sent his own Son into the world and allowed him to be crucified and to die for this. He permitted all the apostles to be persecuted and all Christians to be afflicted for this purpose, and commanded the former faithfully to administer it and the others diligently to hear it. . . .

Let us take it to heart then and remember it, whenever we preach, read, or hear God's word, whether it be in the churches or at home through father, mother, master, or mistress, and gladly believe that wherever we can obtain it we are in the right, high, holy service of God, which pleases him beyond all measure. Thus you will be warmed and stirred to love, hearing it all the more, and God will also grant that it bear fruit, more than anybody can tell. For the word never goes out without bringing forth much fruit whenever it is earnestly heard, without your being the better for it. Even though you do not see it now, in time it will appear. But it would take too long to tell all the fruits now, nor, indeed, can they all be numbered. . . .

What, then, is the sum total of what should be preached? Paul's answer is: "The aim of our charge is love that issues from a pure heart and a good conscience and sincere faith."

There it is; there you have everything in a nutshell, expressed in the finest and fullest way and yet briefly and quickly said and easily retained. This is how you must perform the law if you are going to take hold of it right and seize it by the head, so that you will know what you are to do and not to do, how to submit yourself to it, and not go looking and begging elsewhere and everywhere: You must have the love that flows and issues from a pure heart and a good conscience and sincere faith. You just stick to that! All right preaching starts from there and remains there. He does not do it, Paul is saying, with a doctrine of all kinds of works, in which everything is cut into pieces and peddled. What must be there is what the law really requires, and that is love; the kind of love that flows like a rivulet, a stream, or a spring from a heart which is pure and a good conscience and sincere, unfeigned faith. If that's the way it goes, it's right; if not, then the meaning and sense of the whole law is missed.

Now these are deep and genuinely Pauline words, and besides they are very rich, so we must explain them somewhat, in order to understand it a little and become accustomed to his language. In the first place, he says that the sum of the whole law, that in which it consists and is wholly comprehended, is love. But "love" in German, as everyone knows, means nothing else except to be favorably and affectionately disposed toward a person from the heart and to offer and show him all kindness and friendship. . . .

Love

True love flows from a pure heart. God has commanded me to let my love go out to my neighbor and be kindly disposed to all, whether they be my friends or enemies, just as our heavenly Father himself does. He allows his sun to rise and shine on the good and evil and is most kind to those who are constantly dishonoring him and misusing his goods through disobedience, blasphemy, sin, and shame. He sends rain on the grateful and the selfish (Mt 5:45; Lk 6:35) and gives even to the worst rascals on earth many good things from the earth, and money and possessions besides. Why does he do this? Out of sheer, pure love, of which his heart is full to overflowing, and which he pours out freely over everyone without exception—good or bad, worthy or unworthy. This is a real, divine, total, and perfect love, which does not single out one person nor cut and divide itself, but goes out freely to all.

The other kind of love—when I am a good friend to one who can serve and help me and who esteems me, and hate the one who disregards me and is not on my side—is false love. For it does not issue from a heart which is basically good and pure, the same toward all alike. It comes from a heart which rather seeks only its own and is stuffed full with love for itself and not for others; for it loves nobody except for its own advantage, regards only what will serve it, and seeks in everyone its own profit, not its neighbor's. If you praise and honor that kind of a person, he or she smiles; but if you make a sour face at them or say something they don't like to hear, they flare up, begin to scold and curse, and the friendship is over. . . .

But what is it that makes the heart pure? The answer is that there is no better way of making it pure than through the highest purity, which is God's word. Get that into your heart and order your life by it, and your heart will become pure. For example, take this saying: "You shall love your neighbor as yourself" (Mt 19:19), and order your life by that, and you will see very well whether it will not wash it clean and scour out the selfishness and self-love which is there. For when he commands you to love your neighbor he excludes nobody, neither friend nor enemy, neither good nor evil. For even if people are bad and do evil to you, they do not on that account lose the name of neighbor but remain your flesh and blood and are included in the words, "love your neighbor." Therefore I say to you, if you look at them in the way the word teaches and directs you, your heart will become pure and your love true, so that you will make no false distinction between persons, nor will you look upon them as anything but persons who are good and do good to you. . . .

You see, then, that the word is the cause, foundation, ground, fountain, and spring of love from the heart and of all good works, if they are to please God, for they cannot do so unless the heart first be pure. Even among people works are not acceptable when they are done without the heart in pure hypocrisy. So, if even the emperor and people require the heart, although they cannot see it, how much more does God require a heart which does everything for the sake of the word? That is why he causes his word to be preached, in order that we conform ourselves to it in all our life and action. Let us allow nothing to hinder or trouble us, or make us weak or weary, even though we suffer loss, ingratitude, and contempt because of it, but rather go boldly on and say: I did not begin this for anyone's sake and therefore I will not cease because of people; I shall do it rather for God's sake, let happen what may. This will produce fine people, masters, princes, subjects, preachers, etc., ready to do all good works and to serve and please God with good will and love, for then the fountain and spring is good, not drawn and carried in from the outside. . . .

Conscience

Love should issue from a heart which has a joyful, quiet conscience both toward people and toward God: Toward people in the sense in which Paul boasted that he had so lived that he had neither offended nor grieved anybody nor given a bad example, but that all who saw and heard him were compelled to bear witness that he had served, helped, counselled, and done good to all. Moses too gloried in such a conscience over against his rebellious people, "I have not taken one ass from them, and I have not harmed one of them" (Nm 16:15). Likewise, "Remember how I stood before you to speak good for them, to turn away your wrath from them" (Jer 18:20). And likewise Samuel, "I have walked before you from my youth until this day. Here I am; testify against me before the Lord. . . . Whose ox have I taken? Or whose ass have I taken? Or whom have I defrauded? Whom have I oppressed? Or from whose hand have I taken a bribe to blind my eyes with it? Testify against me and I will restore it to you" (1 Sm 12:2-3).

Look, this is the kind of glory and confidence all Christians should possess. They should so live before everyone and practice and prove their love, that none may bring any complaint against them to terrify and dismay their conscience, but rather that everyone will be truthfully compelled to say that they have so conducted themselves that nothing but improvement has resulted for those who would accept it, and can declare this before God against everyone. This is what it means to have a good conscience toward people or against them.

Even though such a conscience will not be able to stand before God's judgment (any more than the purity of heart which consists in outward life and works of love can stand before him, for before God we still remain sinners), nevertheless we should have this kind of a heart in order that we may comfort ourselves before him and say: This is what God has enjoined and commanded, therefore I do it out of a pure heart and a good conscience, and I would not willingly do otherwise nor offend and hurt anybody; but rather what I say and do is what God has ordered and commanded me to do. . . .

Even though these things are said about our life and our acts, and even though Christians are quite different before God, as we shall hear later, nevertheless they must earnestly endeavor to be blameless before the world. And when they fail to do this, they must interpose the Lord's Prayer and say, both to God and to people, "Forgive us our trespasses, as we forgive those who trespass against us," that so their lives may remain blameless at least before people and retain a good conscience. . . . Then your neighbor will be compelled to say: "Very well, even though you have harmed me or failed to serve me as you should, yet because you have so humbled yourself before me, I will gladly forgive and pardon you, for I too am guilty and I want you to treat me in the same way. For humility's sake, I must admit that you are good, for you do not stubbornly and wilfully insist upon offending me, but rather turn to love." So it can still be called blameless, because it has been covered by humility, and what was blameworthy has been set right, so that none can complain. This is the way the law should be interpreted and preached, in order both that love for every person may rightly proceed from a pure heart for God's sake and that the conscience may stand before the world.

Faith

But in order that all this may be acceptable and stand before God, there is still one other thing that must be added, which is as follows: "and sincere faith."

For, as I have said, even though I have a good conscience before people and practice love from a pure heart, nevertheless there still remains in me the old Adam, the sinful flesh and blood, so that I am not altogether holy and pure. Paul says, "The desires of the Spirit are against the flesh; for these are opposed to each other, to prevent you from doing what you would" (Gal 5:17). And in Romans he says of himself that he must constantly battle and struggle with himself and that he cannot do the good which he would (7:17-24). The Spirit is willing to live purely and perfectly according to God's word, but the flesh remains and resists and tempts us, so that we continue to pursue our own honor, greed, and good days and become slothful, fed up, and weary in our calling.

Thus there remains in us an everlasting strife and resistance, so that much impurity is always creeping in and thus dividing our person, and there can be no flawless purity, or a good conscience, or perfect love, except perhaps what may appear to be so to people. . . .

And here the third part must be added, that is, faith. This is really the chief article and the highest commandment of all, which contains within it all the rest. . . . And it must be a faith which is not hypocritical and mixed with confidence in our own holiness. For wherever this faith is not present, the heart does not become pure before God and the conscience cannot stand when the searching judgment and reckoning begins. Then people will probably let me go in peace and, as far as they are concerned, I may be able to boast that I have served them, preached to them, helped, ruled, and directed them with all faithfulness. And I may say that if I have done too much or too little, I am sorry, for I wanted to do everything I should. Then I shall be safe and excused and they will have nothing more to require of me and will have to wipe the record clean. But here it says bluntly that I must have a pure heart and a good conscience before God, that he may not be able to accuse and condemn me. And this we do not find in ourselves, even though we may have something to boast of before the world. . . .

Here, therefore, the chief article of our doctrine must come to our help: Our Lord Jesus Christ was sent into the world by the Father, suffered and died for us and thereby reconciled and moved the Father to grace, and now sits at the right hand of the Father. He pleads our cause as our Savior and as our constant mediator and intercessor, interceding for us who cannot of ourselves have or obtain this perfect purity and good conscience. Therefore through him we can say before God: Although I am not pure and cannot have a good conscience, yet I cleave to him who possesses perfect purity and good conscience and offers them for me, indeed, gives them to me. . . .

For the scriptures teach me that God established two seats for people: a judgment seat for those who are still secure and proud and will neither acknowledge nor confess their sin, and a mercy seat for those whose conscience is poor and needy, who feel and confess their sin, dread his judgment, and yearn for his grace. And this mercy seat is Christ himself, as Paul says in Romans 3:25, whom God has established for us, that we might have refuge there, since by ourselves we cannot stand before God. . . .

Law and Gospel

We must now learn to distinguish between the two parts which are called the law and the gospel, which is something that we are always teaching. The law brings us before the judgment seat, for it demands that we must be good and that we love out of a pure heart and a good conscience. Its purpose is to make us exercise ourselves in this; so far it must go and then stop. But when it comes and demands that you settle accounts and pay what it requires, there it cancels itself. For even if you have performed what it requires, this still will not stand before God. Before him there will still be much which is lacking and failing, which you have not done and which you do not even realize you have not done. Where will you turn then? The law keeps harrying you and accusing you through your own conscience, which testifies against you, absolutely demanding the judgment upon you. Then you must simply despair, and there is no help or counsel for you unless you know that you can flee from the judgment seat to the mercy seat. . . .

But we teach that one should know and look upon Christ as the one who sits there as the advocate of the poor, terrified conscience. We should believe in him, not as a judge, who is angry and ready to punish, but as a gracious, kindly, comforting mediator between my fearful conscience and God. He says to me: "If you are a sinner and are terrified, and the devil is drawing you to the judgment seat through the law, then come unto me and have no fear of any wrath. Why? Because, if you believe in me, I am sitting here in order that I may step between you and God, so that no wrath or displeasure can touch you; for should wrath and punishment befall you, it must first come upon me." But this is impossible; for he is the beloved Son, in whom all grace dwells, so that when the Father looks upon him, everything in heaven and earth becomes pure love and favor, and all wrath disappears and vanishes away. And whatever he desires and asks of the Father must all be granted without a single doubt or denial. Thus, through faith we are made wholly safe and secure. We shall not be condemned, not because of our holiness or purity, but because of Christ. Because through this faith we cleave to him as our mercy seat, sure that in and with him no wrath can remain, but only love, pardon, and forgiveness. Thus the heart is made pure and the conscience good and secure before God, not out of regard for my own purity or life before the world, but for that lovely treasure which my heart takes hold of, which is my surety and rich store when I am lacking and cannot pay God.

But here is where the emphasis lies—that we must see to it that our faith is not false or, as Paul says, feigned, but rather sincere. For if this fails or proves to be false, then everything fails. For there have always been many, as there still are, who talk a lot about faith and pretend to be masters not only of the law but also of the gospel, and say, as we also say: Faith is what does it, [but then they go on and say] but yet the law and good works must be added to it, otherwise faith does not avail. Thus they mingle together our life and works and Christ. This is not to teach faith purely and sincerely, but is rather faith so colored, feigned, and falsified, that it is not faith at all, but a false semblance and shade of faith, because the confidence of the heart does not rest purely upon Christ as the only mercy seat, but is placed rather in our own holiness, as if this could stand before the judgment seat; wherefore before God it is quite rightly condemned and rejected, which is where it belongs.

For if faith is to be pure, unalloyed, and unfeigned, these two, Christ and my works, must be rightly distinguished. For, after all, everyone must realize that Christ and his work is not my work and life, but something separated from the law and all people's work, far more than one person is different from another. I cannot say that I and the emperor or the pope in Rome are the same thing, and yet I am much nearer and more like them as one mortal, sinful person is to another than to the Lord Christ, who is not only a pure, holy man without any sin whatsoever but also is the one God himself. Therefore let the law and your pure heart and good conscience suffice before people here on earth, but where the mercy seat stands at the right hand of the Father and is the mediator between you and God, there no human work or merit shall have any access or count for anything at all. For what have I or anyone else contributed toward his sitting at the right hand of the Father? He was seated there without any of my work or thought whatsoever and without any co-operation of the law, for there is not a single letter about this in the law. Therefore, he must be cleanly separated from all my being, life, and works and it must be inflexibly concluded that he is something other than our life led before people with a pure heart and good conscience, no matter how good it is. For when that life appears before God and I come before the judgment seat to which the law relegates me, I am condemned and lost. But Christ the mercy seat and those who cleave to him cannot be condemned or convicted. . . .

Therefore, let us hold on to this text, for it is excellently expressed and a pure, perfect teaching of how we are to be righteous both before God and before people, as the law requires, and how these three are to be brought together, a pure heart, a good conscience, and sincere faith, and out of them all our life should flow and continue. Then we shall have found and fulfilled the meaning of the law. But above all, it teaches us that we must look to Christ and bring him into it, who "is the end of the law" (Rom 10:4) and of everything else and our whole righteousness before God.

Basic
Affirmations

Righteousness

As a young monk and priest Luther wrestled with the question, "How can I be right with God?" He learned from the Bible that to be right with God meant to rely totally on faith in Christ, who restores the right relationship with God for all who trust in Christ alone. Paul had summarized what Christ did in Philippians 2:5-11. Luther used verses 5-6 as the biblical basis to preach to his congregation in the Town Church of Wittenberg on the meaning of "righteousness" or "justification" before God. The sermon was preached in 1519. (Source: "Two Kinds of Righteousness," LW 31:297-306.)

Brethren, "have this mind among yourselves, which you have in Christ Jesus, who, though he was in the form of God, did not count equality with God a thing to be grasped" (Phil 2:5-6).

There are two kinds of Christian righteousness, just as sin is of two kinds.

Alien Righteousness

The first is alien righteousness, that is, the righteousness of another, instilled from without. This is the righteousness of Christ by which he justifies through faith, as it is written in 1 Corinthians 1:30: "Whom God made our wisdom, our righteousness and sanctification and redemption." In John 11:25-26, Christ himself states: "I am the resurrection and the life; he who believes in me . . . shall never die." Later he adds in John 14:6, "I am the way, and the truth, and the life." This righteousness, then, is given to us in baptism and whenever we are truly repentant. Therefore we can with confidence boast in Christ and say: "Mine are Christ's living, doing, and speaking, his suffering and dying, mine as much as if I had lived, done, spoken, suffered, and died as he did." Just as a bridegroom possesses all that is his bride's and she all that is his—for the two have all things in common because they are one flesh (Gn 2:24)—so

Christ and the Church are one spirit (Eph 5:29-32). Thus the blessed God and Father of mercies has, according to Peter, granted to us very great and precious gifts in Christ (2 Pt 1:4). Paul writes in 2 Cor 1:3: "Blessed be the God and Father of our Lord Jesus Christ, the Father of mercies and God of all comfort, who has blessed us in Christ with every spiritual blessing in the heavenly places."[1]

This inexpressible grace and blessing was long ago promised to Abraham in Genesis 12:3: "And in your seed (that is, in Christ) shall all the nations of the earth be blessed."[2] Isaiah 9:6 says: "For to us a child is born, to us a son is given." "To us," it says, because he is entirely ours with all his benefits if we believe in him, as we read in Romans 8:32: "He who did not spare his own Son but gave him up for us all, will he not also give us all things with him?" Therefore, everything which Christ has is ours, graciously bestowed on us unworthy people out of God's sheer mercy, although we have rather deserved wrath and condemnation. Even Christ himself, therefore, who says he came to do the most sacred will of his Father (Jn 6:38), became obedient to him; and whatever he did, he did it for us and desired it to be ours, saying, "I am among you as one who serves" (Lk 22:27). He also states, "This is my body, which is given for you" (Lk 22:19). Isaiah 43:24 says, "You have burdened me with your sins, you have wearied me with your iniquities."

Through faith in Christ, therefore, Christ's righteousness becomes our righteousness and all that he has becomes ours; rather, he himself becomes ours. Therefore the apostle calls it "the righteousness of God" in Romans 1:17: For in the gospel "the righteousness of God is revealed . . . as it is written, 'The righteous shall live by his faith.' " Finally, in the same epistle, chapter 3:28, such a faith is called "the righteousness of God": "We hold that a man is justified by faith." This is an infinite

1. The section "who has blessed, etc." is not from 2 Corinthians, as indicated by Luther, but from Ephesians 1:3.

2. Gn 12:3 has "in you" instead of "in your seed." The quotation above is actually from Gn 22:18 (A.V.). Cf. also Gal 3:8.

righteousness, and one that swallows up all sins in a moment, for it is impossible that sin should exist in Christ. On the contrary, who trusts in Christ exists in Christ and is one with Christ, having the same righteousness as he. It is therefore impossible that sin should remain in that person. This righteousness is primary; it is the basis, the cause, the source of all our own actual righteousness. For this is the righteousness given in place of the original righteousness lost in Adam. It accomplishes the same as that original righteousness would have accomplished; rather, it accomplishes more.

It is in this sense that we are to understand the prayer in Psalm 31:1: "In you, O Lord, do I seek refuge; let me never be put to shame; in your righteousness deliver me!" It does not say "in my" but "in your righteousness," that is, in the righteousness of Christ my God, which becomes ours through faith and by the grace and mercy of God. In many passages of the psalter, faith is called "the work of the Lord," "confession," "power of God," "mercy," "truth," "righteousness." All these are names for faith in Christ, rather, for the righteousness which is in Christ. The apostle, therefore, dares to say in Galatians 2:20, "It is no longer I who live, but Christ who lives in me." He further states in Ephesians 3:14-17: "I bow my knees before the Father . . . that . . . he may grant . . . that Christ may dwell in your hearts through faith."

Therefore this alien righteousness, instilled in us without our works by grace alone—while the Father, to be sure, inwardly draws us to Christ—is set opposite original sin, likewise alien, which we acquire without our works by birth alone. Christ daily drives out the old Adam more and more in accordance with the extent to which faith and knowledge of Christ grow. For alien righteousness is not instilled all at once, but it begins, makes progress, and is finally perfected at the end through death.

Proper Righteousness

The second kind of righteousness is our proper righteousness, not because we alone work it, but because we work with that first and alien righteousness. This is that manner of life spent profitably in good works, in the first place, in slaying the flesh and crucifying the desires with respect to the self, of which we read in Galatians 5:24: "And those who belong to Christ Jesus have crucified the flesh with its passions and desires." In the second place, this righteousness consists in love to one's neighbor, and in the third place, in meekness and fear toward God. The apostle is full of references to these, as is all the rest of scripture. He briefly summarizes everything, however, in Titus 2:12: "In this world let us live soberly (pertaining to crucifying one's own flesh), justly (referring to one's neighbor), and devoutly (relating to God)."

This righteousness is the product of the righteousness of the first type, actually its fruit and consequence, for we read in Galatians 5:22: "But the fruit of the spirit is love, joy, peace, patience, kindness, goodness, faithfulness, gentleness, self-control." For because the works mentioned are human works, it is obvious that in this passage a spiritual person is called "spirit." In John 3:6 we read: "That which is born of the flesh is flesh, and that which is born of the Spirit is spirit." This righteousness goes on to complete the first, for it ever strives to do away with the old Adam and to destroy the body of sin. Therefore, it hates itself and loves its neighbor; it does not seek its own good, but that of another, and in this its whole way of living consists. For in that it hates itself and does not seek its own, it crucifies the flesh. Because it seeks the good of another, it works love. Thus in each sphere it does God's will, living soberly with self, justly with neighbor, devoutly toward God.

This righteousness follows the example of Christ in this respect (1 Pt 2:21) and is transformed into his likeness (2 Cor 3:18). It is precisely this that Christ requires. Just as he himself did all things for us, not seeking his own good but ours only—and in this he was most obedient to God the Father—so he desires that we also should set the same example for our neighbors.

We read in Rom 6:19 that this righteousness is set opposite

our own actual sin: "For just as you once yielded your members to impurity and to greater and greater iniquity, so now yield your members to righteousness for sanctification." Therefore, through the first righteousness arises the voice of the bridegroom who says to the soul, "I am yours," but through the second comes the voice of the bride who answers, "I am yours." Then the marriage is consummated; it becomes strong and complete in accordance with the Song of Solomon: "My beloved is mine and I am his" (2:16). Then the soul no longer seeks to be righteous in and for itself, but it has Christ as its righteousness and therefore seeks only the welfare of others. Therefore the Lord of the Synagogue threatens through the prophet, "And I will make to cease from the cities of Judah and from the streets of Jerusalem the voice of mirth and the voice of gladness, the voice of the bridegroom and the voice of the bride" (Jer 7:34).

This is what the text we are now considering says: "Let this mind be in you, which was also in Christ Jesus" (Phil 2:5). This means you should be as inclined and disposed toward one another as you see Christ was disposed toward you. How? Thus, surely, that "though he was in the form of God, [he] did not count equality with God a thing to be grasped, but emptied himself, taking the form of a servant" (Phil 2:6-7). The term "form of God" here does not mean the "essence of God," because Christ never emptied himself of this. Neither can the phrase "form of a servant" be said to mean "human essence." But the "form of God" is wisdom, power, righteousness, goodness—and freedom too; for Christ was a free, powerful, wise man, subject to none of the vices or sins to which all other men are subject. He was pre-eminent in such attributes as are particularly proper to the form of God. Yet, he was not haughty in that form; he did not please himself (Rom 15:3); nor did he disdain and despise those who were enslaved and subjected to various evils.

He was not like the Pharisee who said, "God, I thank you that I am not like other men" (Lk 18:11), for that man was delighted that others were wretched; at any rate he was unwilling that they should be like him. This is the type of robbery by which people usurp things for themselves—rather, they keep what they have and do not clearly ascribe to God the things that are God's, nor do they serve others with them. This kind of people wish to be like God, sufficient in themselves, pleasing themselves, glorying in themselves, under obligation to no one, and so on. Not thus, however, did Christ think; not of this stamp was his wisdom. He relinquished that form to God the Father and emptied himself, unwilling to use his rank against us, unwilling to be different from us. Moreover, for our sakes he became as one of us and took the form of a servant, that is, he subjected himself to all evils. And although he was free, as the apostle says of himself also (1 Cor 9:19), he made himself servant of all (Mk 9:35), living as if all the evils which were ours were actually his own.

Accordingly he took upon himself our sin and our punishment, and although it was for us that he was conquering those things, he acted as though he were conquering them for himself. Although as far as his relationship to us was concerned, he had the power to be our God and Lord, yet he did not will it so, but rather desired to become our servant, as it is written in Romans 15:1, 3: "We . . . ought . . . not to please ourselves. . . . For Christ did not please himself; but, as it is written, 'The reproaches of those who reproached you fell on me' " (Ps 69:9). The quotation from the psalmist has the same meaning as the citation from Paul.

It follows that this passage, which many have understood affirmatively, ought to be understood negatively as follows: That Christ did not count himself equal to God means that he did not wish to be equal to him as those do who presumptuously grasp for equality and say to God, "If you will not give me your glory, I shall seize it for myself." The passage is not to be understood affirmatively as follows: He did not think himself equal to God, that is, the fact that he is equal to God, this he did not consider robbery. For this interpretation is not based on a proper understanding since it speaks of Christ the man. The apostle means that each individual Christian shall become the servant of another in accordance with the example of Christ. If one has wisdom, righteousness, or power with which one can excel others and boast in the "form of God," so to speak, one should not keep all this to oneself, but surrender it to God and become altogether as if one did not possess it (2 Cor 6:10), as one of those who lack it.

Paul's meaning is that when we have forgotten ourselves and emptied ourselves of God's gifts, we should conduct ourselves as if our neighbor's weakness, sin, and foolishness were our very own. We should not boast or get puffed up. Nor should we despise or triumph over our neighbor as if we were his god or equal to God. Since God's prerogatives ought to be left to God alone, it becomes robbery when a person in haughty foolhardiness ignores this fact. It is in this way, then, that one takes the form of a servant, and that command of the apostle in Galatians 5:13 is fulfilled: "Through love be servants of one another." Through the figure of the members of the body Paul teaches in Romans 12:4-5 and 1 Corinthians 12:12-27 how the strong, honorable, healthy members do not glory over those that are weak, less honorable, and sick, as if they were their masters and gods; but on the contrary, they serve them the more, forgetting their own honor, health, and power. For thus no member of the body serves itself; nor does it seek its own welfare but that of the other. And the weaker, the sicker, the less honorable a member is, the more the other members serve it "that there may be no discord in the body, but that the members may have the same care for one another," to use Paul's words (1 Cor 12:25). From this it is now evident how we must conduct ourselves with our neighbor in each situation.

And if we do not freely desire to put off that form of God and take on the form of a servant, let us be compelled to do so against our will. In this regard consider the story in Luke 7:36-50, where Simon the leper, pretending to be in the form of God and perching on his own righteousness, was arrogantly judging and despising Mary Magdalene, seeing in her the form of a servant.

But see how Christ immediately stripped him of that form of righteousness and then clothed him with the form of sin by saying: "You gave me no kiss. . . . You did not anoint my head." How great were the sins that Simon did not see! Nor did he think himself disfigured by such a loathsome form as he had. His good works are not at all remembered.

Christ ignores the form of God in which Simon was superciliously pleasing himself; he does not recount that he was invited, dined, and honored by him. Simon the leper is now nothing but a sinner. He who seemed to himself so righteous sits divested of the glory of the form of God, humiliated in the form of a servant, willy-nilly. On the other hand, Christ honors Mary with the form of God and elevates her above Simon, saying: "She has anointed my feet and kissed them. She has wet my feet with her tears and wiped them with her hair." How great were the merits which neither she nor Simon saw. Her faults are remembered no more. Christ ignored the form of servitude in her whom he has exalted with the form of sovereignty. Mary is nothing but righteous, elevated into the glory of the form of God.

In like manner he will treat all of us whenever we, on the ground of our righteousness, wisdom, or power, are haughty or angry with those who are unrighteous, foolish, or less powerful than we. For when we act thus—and this is the greatest perversion—righteousness works against righteousness, wisdom against wisdom, power against power. For you are powerful, not that you may make the weak weaker by oppression, but that you may make them powerful by raising them up and defending them. You are wise, not in order to laugh at the foolish and thereby make them more foolish, but that you may undertake to teach them as you yourself would wish to be taught. You are righteous that you may vindicate and pardon the unrighteous, not that you may only condemn, disparage, judge, and punish. For this is Christ's example for us, as he says: "For God sent his Son into the world, not to condemn the world, but that the world might be saved through him" (Jn 3:17). He further says in Luke 9:55-56: "You do not know what manner of spirit you are of; for the Son of man came not to destroy men's lives but to save them."

Human Nature

But the carnal, human nature violently rebels, for it greatly delights in punishment, in boasting of its own righteousness, and in its neighbor's shame and embarrassment at his unrighteousness. Therefore it pleads its own case, and it rejoices that this is better than its neighbor's. But it opposes the case of its neighbor and wants it to appear mean. This perversity is wholly evil, contrary to love, which does not seek its own good, but that of another (1 Cor 13:5; Phil 2:4). It ought to be distressed that the condition of its neighbor is not better than its own. It ought to wish that its neighbor's condition were better than its own, and if its neighbor's condition is the better, it ought to rejoice no less than it rejoices when its own is the better. "For this is the law and the prophets" (Mt 7:12).

But you say, "Is it not permissible to chasten an evil person? Is it not proper to punish sin? Who is not obliged to defend righteousness? To do otherwise would give occasion for lawlessness."

I answer: A single solution to this problem cannot be given. Therefore one must distinguish among people. For they can be classified either as public or private individuals.

The things which have been said do not pertain at all to public individuals, that is, to those who have been placed in a responsible office by God. It is their necessary function to punish and judge evil persons, to vindicate and defend the oppressed, because it is not they but God who does this. They are his servants in this very matter, as the apostle shows at some length in Romans 13:4: "He does not bear the sword in vain, etc." But this must be understood as pertaining to the cases of other people, not to one's own. For no one acts in God's place for the sake of himself and his own things, but for the sake of others.

If, however, a public official has a case of his own, let him ask for someone other than himself to be God's representative, for in that case he is not a judge, but one of the parties. But on these matters let others speak at other times, for it is too broad a subject to cover now.

Private individuals with their own cases are of three kinds. First, there are those who seek vengeance and judgment from the representatives of God, and of these there is now a very great number. Paul tolerates such people, but he does not approve of them when he says in 1 Cor 6:12, "All things are lawful for me, but not all things are helpful." Rather he says in the same chapter, "To have lawsuits at all with one another is defeat for you" (1 Cor 6:7). But yet to avoid a greater evil he tolerates this lesser one, lest they should vindicate themselves and one should use force on the other, returning evil for evil, demanding their own advantages. Nevertheless such will not enter the kingdom of heaven unless they have changed for the better by forsaking things that are merely lawful and pursuing those that are helpful. For that passion for one's own advantage must be destroyed.

In the second class are those who do not desire vengeance. On the other hand, in accordance with the gospel, to those who would take their coats, they are prepared to give their cloaks as well, and they do not resist any evil (Mt 5:40). These are children of God, brothers and sisters of Christ, heirs of future blessings. In scripture therefore they are called "fatherless," "widows," "desolate." Because they do not avenge themselves, God wishes to be called their "Father" and "Judge" (Ps 68:5). Far from avenging themselves, if those in authority should wish to seek revenge in their behalf, they either do not desire it or seek it, or they only permit it. Or, if they are among the most advanced, they forbid and prevent it, prepared rather to lose their other possessions also. . . .

In the third class are those who in persuasion are like the second type just mentioned, but are not like them in practice. They are the ones who demand back their own property or seek punishment to be meted out, not because they seek their own advantage, but through the punishment and restoration of their own things they seek the betterment of the one who has stolen or offended. They discern that the offender cannot be improved without punishment. These are called "zealots" and the scriptures praise them. But no one ought to attempt this unless he or she is mature and highly experienced in the second class just mentioned, lest they mistake wrath for zeal and be convicted of doing from anger and impatience that which they believe they are doing from love of justice. For anger is like zeal, and impatience is like love of justice so that they cannot be sufficiently distinguished except by the most spiritual. Christ exhibited such zeal when he made a whip and cast out the sellers and buyers from the temple, as related in John 2:14-17. Paul did likewise when he said, "Shall I come to you with a rod, or with love in a spirit of gentleness?" (1 Cor 4:21).

Freedom

Luther experienced a spiritual breakthrough some time after 1513 when he suffered anxiety through doubts of whether or not God loved him, despite his excellent record as a monk. Reading Paul's Letter to the Romans, and through him the Old Testament prophet Habakkuk, Luther rediscovered the biblical truth that a right relationship with God comes by faith in divine love rather than by merits earned through works of charity (Hab 2:4; Rom 1:17; 3:21-28). Luther felt liberated by this insight. He shared it with fellow friars in conversations, with other theologians in treatises, and with Wittenberg parishioners in sermons. The message was simple yet powerful: Christians are liberated from the bondage of anxiety over sin by faith, given by the Holy Spirit when they rely only on what Christ did for them rather than what they could do to save themselves from the wrath of God. Luther was told by friends to summarize his insight and to communicate it to Rome. For such a view of Christian freedom would be unifying and not dividing. So Luther wrote a treatise in 1520, entitled "The Freedom of the Christian," appending an "Open Letter to Pope Leo X." Both the Latin and German versions of the treatise became quite popular, but there was no response from Rome. (Source: LW 31:333-77.)

Many people have considered Christian faith an easy thing, and not a few have given it a place among the virtues. They do this because they have not experienced it and have never tasted the great strength there is in faith. It is impossible to write well about it or to understand what has been written about it unless one has at one time or another experienced the courage which faith gives persons when trials oppress them. But who has had even a faint taste of it can never write, speak, meditate, or hear enough concerning it. It is a living "spring of water welling up to eternal life," as Christ calls it in John 4:14.

As for me, although I have no wealth of faith to boast of and know how scant my supply is, I nevertheless hope that I have attained to a little faith, even though I have been assailed by great and various temptations. . . .

To make the way smoother for the unlearned—for only them

do I serve—I shall set down the following two propositions concerning the freedom and the bondage of the spirit:

A Christian is a perfectly free lord of all, subject to none.

A Christian is a perfectly dutiful servant of all, subject to all.

These two theses seem to contradict each other. If, however, they should be found to fit together they would serve our purpose beautifully. Both are Paul's own statements, who says in 1 Corinthians 9:19, "For though I am free from all men, I have made myself a slave to all," and in Romans 13:8, "Owe no one anything, except to love one another." Love by its very nature is ready to serve and be subject to him who is loved. So Christ, although he was Lord of all, was "born of woman, born under the law" (Gal 4:4), and therefore was at the same time a free man and a servant, "in the form of God" and "of a servant" (Phil 2:6-7).

Let us start, however, with something more remote from our subject, but more obvious. There is a twofold human nature, a spiritual and a bodily one. According to the spiritual nature, which we refer to as the soul, we are called a spiritual, inner, or new human being. According to the bodily nature, which we refer to as flesh, we are called a carnal, outward, or old being, of whom the apostle writes in 2 Corinthians 4:16, "Though our outer nature is wasting away, our inner nature is being renewed every day." Because of this diversity of nature the scriptures assert contradictory things concerning the same human being, since these two natures in the same being contradict each other, "for the desires of the flesh are against the Spirit, and the desires of the Spirit are against the flesh," according to Galatians 5:17.

The Birth of Freedom

First, let us consider the inner human being to see how a righteous, free, and pious Christian, that is, a spiritual, new, and inner being, becomes what he or she is. It is evident that no external thing has any influence in producing Christian righteousness or freedom, or in producing unrighteousness or servitude. A simple argument will furnish the proof of this statement. What can it profit the soul if the body is well, free, and active, and eats, drinks, and does as it pleases? For in these respects even the most godless slaves of vice may prosper. On the other hand, how will poor health or imprisonment or hunger or thirst or any other external misfortune harm the soul? Even the most godly people, and those who are free because of clear consciences, are afflicted with these things. None of these things touch either the freedom or the servitude of the soul. It does not help the soul if the body is adorned with the sacred robes of priests or dwells in sacred places or is occupied with sacred duties or prays, fasts, abstains from certain kinds of food, or does any work that can be done by the body and in the body. The righteousness and the freedom of the soul require something far different, since the things which have been mentioned could be done by any wicked person. Such works produce nothing but hypocrites. On the other hand, it will not harm the soul if the body is clothed in secular dress, dwells in unconsecrated places, eats and drinks as others do, does not pray aloud, and neglects to do all the above-mentioned things which hypocrites can do.

Furthermore, to put aside all kinds of works, even contemplation, meditation, and all that the soul can do, does not help. One thing, and only one thing, is necessary for Christian life, righteousness, and freedom. That one thing is the most holy word of God, the gospel of Christ, as Christ says in John 11:25, "I am the resurrection and the life; he who believes in me, though he die, yet shall he live"; and John 8:36, "So if the Son makes you free, you will be free indeed"; and Matthew 4:4, "One shall not live by bread alone, but by every word that proceeds from the mouth of God."

Let us then consider it certain and firmly established that the soul can do without anything except the word of God, and that where the word of God is missing there is no help at all for the soul. If it has the word of God, it is rich and lacks nothing, since it is the word of life, truth, light, peace, righteousness, salvation, joy, liberty, wisdom, power, grace, glory, and of every incalculable blessing. This is why the prophet in the entire Psalm 119 and in many other places yearns and sighs for the word of God and uses so many names to describe it.

On the other hand, there is no more terrible disaster with which the wrath of God can afflict people than a famine of the hearing of his word, as he says in Amos (8:11). Likewise there is no greater mercy than when he sends forth his word, as we read in Psalm 107:20: "He sent forth his word, and healed them, and delivered them from destruction." Nor was Christ sent into the world for any other ministry except that of the word. Moreover, the entire spiritual estate—all the apostles, bishops, and priests—has been called and instituted only for the ministry of the word.

You may ask, "What then is the word of God, and how shall it be used, since there are so many words of God?" I answer: The apostle explains this in Romans 1. The word is the gospel of God concerning his Son, who was made flesh, suffered, rose from the dead, and was glorified through the Spirit who sanctifies. To preach Christ means to feed the soul, make it righteous, set it free, and save it, provided it believes the preaching. Faith alone is the saving and efficacious use of the word of God, according to Romans 10:9: "If you confess with your lips that Jesus is Lord and believe in your heart that God raised him from the dead, you will be saved." Furthermore, "Christ is the end of the law, that everyone who has faith may be justified" (Rom 10:4). Again, in Romans 1:17, "He who through faith is righteous shall live." The word of God cannot be received and cherished by any works whatever but only by faith. Therefore it is clear that, as the soul needs only the word of God for its life and righteousness, so it is justified by faith alone and not by any works; for if it could be justified by anything else, it would not need the word, and consequently it would not need faith.

This faith cannot exist in connection with works, that is to say, if you at the same time claim to be justified by works, whatever their character. For that would be the same as "limping with two different opinions" (1 Kgs 18:21), as worshiping Baal and kissing one's own hand (Jb 31:27-28), which, as Job says, is a very great iniquity. Therefore, the moment you begin to have faith you learn that all things in you are altogether blameworthy, sinful, and damnable, as the apostle says in Romans 3:23, "Since all have sinned and fall short of the glory of God," and, "None is righteous, no, not one . . . all have turned aside, together they have gone wrong" (Rom 3:10-12). When you have learned this you will know that you need Christ, who suffered and rose again for you so that, if you believe in him, you may through this faith become a new man insofar as your sins are forgiven and you are justified by the merits of another, namely, of Christ alone.

Since, therefore, this faith can rule only in the inner human being, as Romans 10:10 says, "For one believes with the heart and so is justified," and since faith alone justifies, it is clear that the inner being cannot be justified, freed, or saved by any outer work or action at all, and that these works, whatever their character, have nothing to do with this inner being. On the other hand, only ungodliness and unbelief of heart, and no outer work, make us guilty and a damnable servant of sin. Wherefore it ought to be the first concern of every Christian to lay aside all confidence in works and increasingly to strengthen faith alone, and through faith to grow in the knowledge, not of works, but of Christ Jesus, who suffered and rose for him, as Peter teaches in the last chapter of his first epistle (1 Pt 5:10). No other work makes a Christian. Thus, when the Jews asked Christ, as related in John 6:28, what they must do "to be doing the work of God," he brushed aside the multitude of works, which he saw they did in great profusion, and suggested one work, saying, "This is the work of God, that you believe in him whom he has sent" (Jn 6:27).

Therefore, true faith in Christ is a treasure beyond comparison, which brings with it complete salvation and saves us from every evil, as Christ says in the last chapter of Mark: "He who believes and is baptized will be saved; but he who does not believe will be condemned" (16:16). Isaiah contemplated this treasure and foretold it in chapter 10:22: "Destruction is decreed, overflowing with righteousness." This is as though he said, "Faith, which is a small and perfect fulfilment of the law, will fill believers with so great a righteousness that they will need nothing more to become righteous." So Paul says in Romans 10:10, "For one believes with the heart and so is justified."

Mandates and Promises

Should you ask how it happens that faith alone justifies and offers us such a treasure of great benefits without works, in view of the fact that so many works, ceremonies, and laws are prescribed in the scriptures, I answer: First of all, remember what has been said, namely, that faith alone, without works, justifies, frees, and saves; we shall make this clearer later on. Here we must point out that the entire scripture of God is divided into two parts: commandments and promises. Although the commandments teach things that are good, the things taught are not done as soon as they are taught, for the commandments show us what we ought to do but do not give us the power to do it. They are intended to teach us to know ourselves, that through them we may recognize our inability to do good and may despair of our own ability. That is why they are called the Old Testament and constitute the Old Testament. For example, the commandment, "You shall not covet" (Ex 20:17), is a command which proves us all to be sinners, for no one can avoid coveting no matter how much he or she may struggle against it. Therefore, in order not to covet and to fulfill the commandment, we are compelled to despair of ourselves, to seek the help which we do not find in ourselves elsewhere and from someone else, as stated in Hosea: "Destruction is your own, O Israel: your help is only in me" (13:9). As we fare with respect to one commandment, so we fare with all, for it is equally impossible for us to keep any one of them.

Now when we have learned through the commandments to recognize our helplessness and are distressed about how we might satisfy the law—since the law must be fulfilled so that not a jot or tittle shall be lost, otherwise we will be condemned without hope—then, being truly humbled and reduced to nothing in our own eyes, we find in ourselves nothing whereby we may be justified and saved. Here the second part of scripture comes to our aid, namely, the promises of God which declare the glory of God, saying, "If you wish to fulfill the law and not covet, as the law demands, come, believe in Christ in whom grace, righteousness, peace, liberty, and all things are promised you. If you believe, you shall have all things; if you do not believe, you shall lack all things." That which is impossible for you to accomplish by trying to fulfill all the works of the law—many and useless as they all are—you will accomplish quickly and easily through faith. God our Father has made all things depend on faith so that whoever has faith will have everything, and whoever does not have faith will have nothing. "For God has consigned all to disobedience, that he may have mercy upon all," as it is stated in Romans 11:32. Thus the promises of God give what the commandments of God demand and fulfill what the law prescribes so that all things may be God's alone, both the commandments and the fulfilling of the commandments. He alone commands, he alone fulfills. Therefore the promises of God belong to the New Testament. Indeed, they are the New Testament.

Since these promises of God are holy, true, righteous, free, and peaceful words, full of goodness, the soul which clings to them with a firm faith will be so closely united with them and altogether absorbed by them that it not only will share in all their power but will be saturated and intoxicated by them. If a touch of Christ healed, how much more will this most tender spiritual touch, this absorbing of the word, communicate to the soul all things that belong to the word. This, then, is how through faith alone without works the soul is justified by the word of God, sanctified, made true, peaceful, and free, filled with every blessing and truly made a child of God, as John 1:12 says: "But to all who . . . believed in his name, he gave power to become children of God."

The Power of Faith

From what has been said it is easy to see from what source faith derives such great power and why a good work or all good works together cannot equal it. No good work can rely upon the word of God or live in the soul, for faith alone and the word of God rule in the soul. Just as the heated iron glows like fire because of the union of fire with it, so the word imparts its qualities to the soul. It is clear, then, that Christians have all that they need in faith and need no works to justify them; and if they have no need of works, they have no need of the law; and if they have no need of the law, surely they are free from the law. It is true that "the law is not laid down for the just" (1 Tm 1:9). This is that Christian liberty, our faith, which does not induce us to live in idleness or wickedness but makes the law and works unnecessary for anyone's righteousness and salvation.

This is the first power of faith. Let us now examine also the second. It is a further function of faith that it honors those whom it trusts with the most reverent and highest regard since it considers them truthful and trustworthy. There is no other honor equal to the estimate of truthfulness and righteousness with which we honor those whom we trust. Could we ascribe to a person anything greater than truthfulness and righteousness and perfect goodness? On the other hand, there is no way in which we can show greater contempt for people than to regard them as false and wicked and to be suspicious of them, as we do when we do not trust them. So when the soul firmly trusts God's promises, it regards him as truthful and righteous. Nothing more excellent than this can be ascribed to God. The very highest worship of God is that we ascribe to him truthfulness, righteousness, and whatever else should be ascribed to one who is trusted. When this is done, the soul consents to his will. Then it hallows his name and allows itself to be treated according to God's good pleasure for, clinging to God's promises, it does not doubt that he who is true, just, and wise will do, dispose, and provide all things well. . . .

The third incomparable benefit of faith is that it unites the soul with Christ, as a bride is united with her bridegroom. By this mystery, as the apostle teaches, Christ and the soul become one flesh (Eph 5:31-32). And if they are one flesh and there is between them a true marriage—indeed the most perfect of all marriages, since human marriages are but poor examples of this one true marriage—it follows that everything they have they hold in common, the good as well as the evil. Accordingly the believing soul can boast of and glory in whatever Christ has as though it were its own, and whatever the soul has Christ claims as his own. Let us compare these and we shall see inestimable benefits. Christ is full of grace, life, and salvation. The soul is full of sins, death, and damnation. Now let faith come between them and sins, death, and damnation will be Christ's, while grace, life, and salvation will be the soul's; for if Christ is a bridegroom, he must take upon himself the things which are his bride's and bestow upon her the things that are his. If he gives her his body and very self, how shall he not give her all that is his? And if he takes the body of the bride, how shall he not take all that is hers?

Here we have a most pleasing vision not only of communion but of a blessed struggle and victory and salvation and redemption. Christ is God and man in one person. He has neither sinned nor died and is not condemned; and he cannot sin, die, or be condemned; his righteousness, life, and salvation are unconquerable, eternal, omnipotent. By the wedding ring of faith he shares in the sins, death, and pains of hell which are his bride's. As a matter of fact, he makes them his own and acts as if they were his own and as if he himself had sinned; he suffered, died, and descended into hell that he might overcome them all. Now since it was such a one who did all this, and death and hell could not swallow him up, these were necessarily swallowed up by

him in a mighty duel; for his righteousness is greater than the
sins of all people, his life stronger than death, his salvation more
invincible than hell. Thus, by means of the pledge of its faith,
the believing soul is free in Christ, its bridegroom, free from all
sins, secure against death and hell, and is endowed with the
eternal righteousness, life, and salvation of Christ it's
bridgroom. So he takes to himself a glorious bride, "without
spot or wrinkle, cleansing her by the washing of water with the
word" of life (Eph 5:26-27), that is, by faith in the word of life,
righteousness, and salvation. In this way he marries her in faith,
steadfast love, and in mercies, righteousness, and justice, as
Hosea 2:19-20 says.

Who then can fully appreciate what this royal marriage
means? Who can understand the riches of the glory of this
grace? Here this rich and divine bridegroom Christ marries this
poor, wicked harlot, redeems her from all her evil, and adorns
her with all his goodness. Her sins cannot now destroy her, since
they are laid upon Christ and swallowed up by him. And she
has that righteouness in Christ, her husband, of which she may
boast as of her own and which she can confidently display
alongside her sins in the face of death and hell and say, "If I have
sinned, yet my Christ, in whom I believe, has not sinned, and
all his is mine and all mine is his," as the bride in the song of
Solomon says, "My beloved is mine and I am his" (2:16). This is
what Paul means when he says in 1 Corinthians 15:57, "Thanks
be to God, who gives us the victory through our Lord Jesus
Christ," that is, the victory over sin and death, as he also says
there, "The sting of death is sin, and the power of sin is the law"
(1 Cor 15:56).

From this you once more see that much is ascribed to faith,
namely, that it alone can fulfill the law and justify without
works. . . .

Now let us turn to the second part, the outer human being.
Here we shall answer all those who, offended by the word
"faith" and by all that has been said, now ask, "If faith does all
things and is alone sufficient unto righteousness, why then are

good works commanded? We will take our ease and do no works and be content with faith. . . ." That would indeed be proper if we were wholly inner and perfectly spiritual beings. But such we shall be only at the last day, the day of the resurrection of the dead. As long as we live in the flesh we only begin to make some progress in that which shall be perfected in the future life. For this reason the apostle in Romans 8:23 calls all that we attain in this life "the first fruits of the Spirit," because we shall indeed receive the greater portion, even the fullness of the Spirit, in the future. This is the place to assert that which was said above, namely, that Christians are the servants of all and made subject to all. Insofar as they are free they do no works, but insofar as they are servants they do all kinds of works. How this is possible we shall see.

Although, as I have said, we are abundantly and sufficiently justified by faith inwardly, in our spirit, and so have all that we need, except insofar as this faith and these riches must grow from day to day even to the future life; yet we remain in this mortal life on earth. In this life he must control our own body and have dealings with people. Here the works begin; here we cannot enjoy leisure; here we must indeed take care to discipline our body by fastings, watchings, labors, and other reasonable discipline, and to subject it to the Spirit so that it will obey and conform to the inner being and faith and not revolt against faith and hinder the inner being, as it is the nature of the body to do if it is not held in check. The inner being, who by faith is created in the image of God, is both joyful and happy because of Christ in whom so many benefits are conferred upon him; and therefore it is our one occupation to serve God joyfully and without thought of gain, in love that is not constrained.

While we are doing this, behold, we meet a contrary will in our own flesh, which strives to serve the world and seeks its own advantage. This the spirit of faith cannot tolerate, but with joyful zeal it attempts to put the body under control and hold it in check, as Paul says in Romans 7:22-23, "For I delight in the law of God, in my inmost self, but I see in my members another law at war with the law of my mind and making me captive to the law of sin," and in another place, "But I pommel my body and subdue it, lest after preaching to others I myself should be disqualified" (1 Cor 9:27), and in Galatians, "And those who belong to Christ Jesus have crucified the flesh with its passions and desires" (5:24).

Christians live not in themselves, but in Christ and in their neighbors. Otherwise they are not Christians. They live in Christ through faith, in their neighbor through love. By faith they are caught up beyond themselves into God. By love they descend beneath themselves into their neighbor. Yet, they always remain in God and in his love, as Christ says in John 1:51, "Truly, truly, I say to you, you will see heaven opened, and the angels of God ascending and descending upon the Son of man."

Church

Luther alerted people to the third article of the three ecumenical creeds (Apostles', Nicene, Athanasian) when there was a question about the Church. Accordingly, he preferred to speak of the Chuch as "the communion of saints," that is, people called by the Holy Spirit who makes them "holy"—called to give testimony to God's love in Christ for the world. In order to obey this calling, the Church had developed a hierarchy of leadership, with the final authority assigned to a "general" or "ecumenical council" of bishops; in the Western Church such a council was chaired by the pope. Luther accepted the authority of the council, but without papal leadership (as is the case in the Eastern "Orthodox" Church). He and others in his reform movement called for such a council to settle the increasing differences between the "reformers" and the defenders of the status quo. To clarify his stance, Luther wrote a lengthy treatise in 1539, "On the Councils and the Church," dealing with the questions of what a true council is, how earlier councils are to be judged, and what the marks of the true Church are. These questions are still controversial today, given the different ways in which Church authority is exercised in various Christian communions. Luther lists seven identifying marks of the Church that establish its authority. Besides these marks, there are other "externals" that represent human efforts to ensure the mission of the Church in the world—institutional structure, forms of worship, and other "outward things." The selections are taken from the third part of the treatise. (Source: LW 41:148-66.)

Seven Marks

The Creed teaches us that a Christian holy people is to be and to remain on earth until the end of the world. This is an article of faith that cannot be terminated until that which it believes comes, as Christ promises, "I am with you always, to the close of the age" (Mt 28:20). But how will or how can a poor confused person tell where such Christian holy people are to be found in this world? Indeed, they are supposed to be in this life and on earth, for they of course believe that a heavenly nature and an eternal life are to come, but as yet they do not possess them. Therefore, they must still be in this life and remain in this life

106

and in this world until the end of the world. For they profess, "I believe in another life"; thereby they confess that they have not yet arrived in the other life, but believe in it, hope for it, and love it as their true fatherland and life, while they must yet remain and tarry here in exile—as we sing in the hymn about the Holy Spirit, "As homeward we journey from this exile. Lord, have mercy."[1] We shall now speak of this.

First, the holy Christian people are recognized by their possession of the holy word of God. To be sure, not all have it in equal measure, as Paul says (1 Cor 3:12-14). Some possess the word in its complete purity, others do not. Those who have the pure word are called those who "build on the foundation with gold, silver, and precious stones"; those who do not have it in its purity are the ones who "build on the foundation with wood, hay, and straw," and yet will be saved through fire. . . . This is the principal item, and the holiest of holy possessions,[2] by reason of which the Christian people are called holy; for God's word is holy and sanctifies everything it touches; it is indeed the very holiness of God. "It is the power of God for salvation to everyone who has faith" (Rom 1:16) and "Everything is consecrated by the word of God and prayer" (1 Tm 4:5). For the Holy Spirit himself administers it and anoints or sanctifies the Christian Church with it. . . .

We are speaking of the external word, preached orally by people like you and me, for this is what Christ left behind as an external sign, by which his Church, or his Christian people in the world, should be recognized. We also speak of this external word as it is sincerely believed and openly professed before the world, as Christ says, "Everyone who acknowledges me before others, I also will acknowledge before my Father and his angels" (Mt 10:32). There are many who know it in their hearts but will not

---

1. The fourth line of a pre-Reformation hymn adapted by Luther in 1524, "Now Let Us Pray to the Holy Ghost." (LW 53, 263-64.)

2. *Heiligthum* or *Heilthum.* These words recur continually in the following section. The term "holy possession" conveys both the meaning of "sanctuary" and "relic." Luther plays constantly on the idea of wonder-working objects of reverence when he speaks of the marks of the Church.

profess it openly. Many possess it, but do not believe in it or act by it, for the number of those who believe in and act by it is small—as the parable of the seed in Matthew 13:4-8 says that three sections of the field receive and contain the seed, but only the fourth section, the fine and good soil, bears fruit with patience.

Now, wherever you hear or see this word preached, believed, professed, and lived, do not doubt that the true *ecclesia sancta catholica*, "a Christian holy people" must be there, even though their number is very small. For God's word "shall not return empty" (Is 55:11), but must have at least a fourth or a fraction of the field. And even if there were no other sign than this alone, it would still suffice to prove that a Christian, holy people must exist there, for God's word cannot be without God's people, and conversely, God's people cannot be without God's word. Otherwise, who would preach or hear it preached, if there were no people of God? And what could or would God's people believe, if there were no word of God? . . .

Second, God's people or the Christian holy people are recognized by the holy sacrament of baptism, wherever it is taught, believed, and administered correctly according to Christ's ordinance. That too is a public sign and a precious, holy possession by which God's people are sanctified. It is the holy bath of regeneration through the Holy Spirit (Ti 3:5), in which we bathe and with which we are washed of sin and death by the Holy Spirit, as in the innocent holy blood of the Lamb of God. Wherever you see this sign you may know that the Church, or the holy Christian people, must surely be present, even if the pope does not baptize you or even if you know nothing of his holiness and power—just as the little children know nothing of it, although when they are grown, they are, sad to say, estranged from their baptism, as Peter laments in 2 Peter 2:18, "They entice with licentious passions of the flesh people who have barely escaped from those who live in error," etc. Indeed, you should not even pay attention to who baptizes, for baptism does not belong to the baptizer, nor is it given to him, but it belongs to the baptized. It was ordained for him by God and given to him by God, just as the word of God is not the preacher's (except insofar as he too hears and believes it) but belongs to the disciple who hears and believes it; to him or her is it given.

Third, God's people, or Christian holy people, are recognized by the holy sacrament of the altar, wherever it is rightly administered, believed, and received, according to Christ's institution. This too is a public sign and a precious, holy possession left behind by Christ by which his people are sanctified so that they also exercise themselves in faith and openly confess that they are Christians, just as they do with the word and with baptism. And here too you need not be disturbed if the pope does not say Mass for you, does not consecrate, anoint, or vest you with a chasuble. Indeed, you may, like a patient in bed, receive this sacrament without wearing any garb, except that outward decency obliges you to be properly covered. Moreover, you need not ask whether you have a tonsure or are anointed. In addition, the question of whether you are male or female, young or old, need not be argued—just as little as it matters in baptism and the preached word. It is enough that you are consecrated and anointed with the sublime and holy chrism of God, with the word of God, with baptism, and also this sacrament; then you are anointed highly and gloriously enough and sufficiently vested with priestly garments. . . .

Wherever you see this sacrament properly administered, there you may be assured of the presence of God's people. For, as was said above of the word, wherever God's word is, there the Church must be; likewise, wherever baptism and the sacrament are, God's people must be, and vice versa. No others have, give, practice, use, and confess these holy possessions save God's people alone, even though some false and unbelieving Christians are secretly among them. They, however, do not profane the people of God because they are not known; the Church, or God's people, does not tolerate known sinners in its midst, but reproves them and also makes them holy. Or, if they refuse, it casts them out from the sanctuary by means of the ban and regards them as heathen (Mt 18:17).

Fourth, God's people or holy Christians are recognized by the office of the keys exercised publicly. That is, as Christ decrees in Matthew 18:15-20, if Christians sin, they should be reproved; and if they don't mend their ways, they should be bound in their sin and cast out. If they do mend their ways, they should be absolved. That is the office of the keys. Now the use of the keys is twofold, public and private. There are some people with consciences so tender and despairing that even if they have not been publicly condemned, they cannot find comfort until they have been individually absolved by the pastor. On the other hand, there are also some who are so obdurate that they neither recant in their heart and want their sins forgiven individually by the pastor, nor desist from their sins. Therefore the keys must be used differently, publicly and privately. Now where you see sins forgiven or reproved in some persons, be it publicly or privately, you may know that God's people are there. If God's people are not there, the keys are not there either; and if the keys are not present for Christ, God's people are not present. Christ bequeathed them as a public sign and a holy possession, whereby the Holy Spirit again sanctifies the fallen sinners redeemed by Christ's death, and whereby the Christians confess that they are a holy people in this world under Christ. . . .

Fifth, the Church is recognized externally by the fact that it consecrates or calls ministers, or has offices that it is to administer. There must be bishops, pastors, or preachers, who publicly and privately give, administer, and use the aforementioned four things or holy possessions in behalf of and in the name of the Church, or rather by reason of their institution by Christ, as Paul states in Ephesians 4:8, "He received gifts among men."[3]—his gifts were that some should be apostles, some prophets, some evangelists, some teachers and governors, etc. The people as a whole cannot do these things, but must entrust or have them entrusted to one person. Otherwise, what would happen if everyone wanted to speak or administer, and no one wanted to

---

3. Luther is as usual quoting from memory, and confuses Eph 4:8 with Ps 68:18, from which the Ephesian passage quotes.

give way to the other? It must be entrusted to one person, and that one alone should be allowed to preach, to baptize, to absolve, and to administer the sacraments. The others should be content with this arrangement and agree to it. Wherever you see this done, be assured that God's people, the holy Christian people, are present. . . .

Just as was said earlier about the other four parts of the great, divine, holy possession by which the holy Church is sanctified, that you need not care who or how those from whom you receive it are, so again you should not ask who and how he is who gives it to you or has the office. For all of it is given, not to who has the office, but to who is to receive it through this office, except that he or she can receive it together with you if he or she so desires. Let him be what he will. Because he is in office and is tolerated by the assembly, you put up with him too. His person will make God's word and sacraments neither worse nor better for you. What he says or does is not his, but Christ, your Lord, and the Holy Spirit say and do everything, insofar as he adheres to correct doctrine and practice. The Church, of course, cannot and should not tolerate open vices; but you yourself be content and tolerant, since you, an individual, cannot be the whole assembly or the Christian holy people.

Sixth, the holy Christian people are externally recognized by prayer, public praise, and thanksgiving to God. Where you see and hear the Lord's Prayer prayed and taught; or psalms or other spiritual songs sung, in accordance with the word of God and the true faith; also the creed, the ten commandments, and the catechism used in public, you may rest assured that a holy Christian people of God are present. For prayer, too, is one of the precious holy possessions whereby everything is sanctified, as Paul says (1 Tm 4:5). The psalms too are nothing but prayers in which we praise, thank, and glorify God. The creed and the ten commandments are also God's word and belong to the holy possession, whereby the Holy Spirit sanctifies the holy people of Christ. . . .

Seventh, the holy Christian people are externally recognized by the holy possession of the sacred cross. They must endure every misfortune and persecution, all kinds of trials and evil from the devil, the world, and the flesh (as the Lord's Prayer indicates) by inward sadness, timidity, fear, outward poverty, contempt, illness, and weakness, in order to become like their head, Christ. And the only reason they must suffer is that they steadfastly adhere to Christ and God's word, enduring this for the sake of Christ. "Blessed are you when they persecute you on my account" (Mt 5:11). They must be pious, quiet, obedient, and prepared to serve the government and everybody with life and goods, doing no one any harm. No people on earth have to endure such bitter hate. . . . In summary, they must be called heretics, knaves, and devils, the most pernicious people on earth, to the point where those who hang, drown, murder, torture, banish, and plague them to death are rendering God a service. No one has compassion on them; they are given myrrh and gall to drink when they thirst. And all of this is done not because they are adulterers, murderers, thieves, or rogues, but because they want to have none but Christ, and no other god. Wherever you see or hear this, you may know that the holy Christian Church is there, as Christ says in Matthew "Blessed are you when they revile you and utter all kinds of evil against you on my account. Rejoice and be glad, for your reward is great in heaven" (5:11-12). This too is a holy possession whereby the Holy Spirit not only sanctifies his people, but also blesses them.

These are the true seven principal parts of the great holy possession whereby the Holy Spirit effects in us a daily sanctification and vivification in Christ, according to the first table of Moses. By this we obey it, albeit never as perfectly as Christ. But we constantly strive to attain the goal, under his redemption or remission of sin, until we too shall one day become perfectly holy and no longer stand in need of forgiveness. Everything is directed toward that goal. . . .

Other Signs

In addition to these seven principal parts there are other outward signs that identify the Christian Church, namely, those things whereby the Holy Spirit sanctifies us according to the second table of Moses; when he assists us in sincerely honoring our father and mother, and conversely, when he helps them to raise their children in a Christian way and to lead honorable lives; when we faithfully serve our princes and lords and are obedient and subject to them, and conversely, when they love their subjects and protect and guard them; also when we bear no one a grudge, entertain no anger, hatred, envy, or vengefulness toward our neighbors, but gladly forgive them, lend to them, help them, and counsel them; when we are not lewd, not drunkards, not proud, arrogant, overbearing, but chaste, self-controlled, sober, friendly, kind, gentle, and humble; when we do not steal, rob, are not usurious, greedy, do not overcharge, but are mild, kind, content, charitable; when we are not false, mendacious, perjurers, but truthful, trustworthy, and do whatever else is taught in these commandments—all of which Paul teaches abundantly in more than one place. We need the Decalogue not only to apprise us of our lawful obligations, but we also need it to discern how far the Holy Spirit has advanced us in his work of sanctification and by how much we still fall short of the goal, lest we become secure and imagine that we have now done all that is required. Thus we must constantly grow in sanctification and always become new creatures in Christ. This means "grow" and "do so more and more" (2 Pt 3:18).

However, these signs cannot be regarded as being as reliable as those noted before, since some heathens too practice these works and indeed at times appear holier than Christians; yet their actions do not issue from the heart purely and simply, for the sake of God, but they search for some other end, because they lack a real faith in and a true knowledge of God. But here is the Holy Spirit, who sanctifies the heart and produces these fruits from "an honest and good heart" (Lk 8:15). Since the first table is greater and must be a holier possession, I have summarized everything in the second table. Otherwise, I could have divided it too into seven holy possessions or seven principal parts, according to the seven commandments.

Personal Confession

Luther wanted to be known as a defender of Christian unity, not as a schismatic or heretic. The reform movement in Switzerland, led by Ulrich Zwingli since 1522 in Zurich, rejected basic Christian truths, such as the presence of Christ in the eucharist. Luther's opponents tried to link him with Zwingli. Luther, however, made it clear that Zwingli was a radical who preached a disembodied gospel by rejecting the sacrament of holy communion. He called Zwingli and other radicals "swarmers" (*Schwaermer*) who, like wild bees, disturbed and threatened Christian unity. That is why Luther wrote angry treatises against Zwingli and other *Schwaermer*, the longest being his "Confession Concerning the Lord's Supper" in 1528. In it, Luther used lengthy arguments to refute Zwingli's view of the eucharist as a "memorial" of Christ's death, to be celebrated only on high festivals, such as Christmas and Easter. Part I of the treatise attacks Zwingli's philosophical presuppositions; part II refutes his interpretation of biblical texts; and part III offers a confession of faith to show Luther's ecumenical stance, based on the trinitarian creeds. The selections are taken from part III. (Source: LW 37:360-72.)

I desire with this treatise to confess my faith before God and all the world, point by point. I am determined to abide by it until my death and (so help me God!) in this faith to depart from this world and to appear before the judgment seat of our Lord Jesus Christ. . . .

God, the Father

I believe with my whole heart the sublime article of the majesty of God, that the Father, Son, and Holy Spirit, three distinct persons, are by nature one true and genuine God, the maker of heaven and earth; in complete opposition to the Arians, Macedonians, Sabellians,[1] and similar heretics. All this has

---

1. Macedonianism, named after Macedonius, a fourth-century archbishop of Constantinople, affirmed that the Holy Spirit is less than divine, not one of the divine persons; this view was condemned at a council at Alexandria in 362 and

been maintained up to this time both in the Roman Church and among Christian Churches throughout the whole world.

God, the Son

I believe and know that scripture teaches us that the second person in the Godhead, that is, the Son, alone became true man, conceived by the Holy Spirit without human co-operation, and was born of the pure, holy Virgin Mary as of a real natural mother, all of which Luke clearly describes and the prophets foretold, so that neither the Father nor the Holy Spirit became man, as certain heretics have taught.[2]

Also that God the son assumed not a body without a soul, as certain heretics have taught,[3] but also the soul, that is, full, complete humanity, and was born the promised true seed or child of Abraham and of David and the son of Mary by nature, in every way and form a true man, as I am myself and every other man, except that he came without sin, by the Holy Spirit of the Virgin Mary alone.

And that this man became true God, as one eternal, indivisible person, of God and man, so that Mary the holy Virgin is a real, true mother not only of the man Christ, as the Nestorians teach,[4] but also of the Son of God, as Luke says, "The child to be

---

subsequently. Sabellianism, a third century form of Modal Monarchianism, treated the terms Father, Son, and Holy Spirit not as distinct divine persons but simply as different modes or even successive phases of the one God. It was Arius' accusation of Sabellianism against his bishop which opened the controversy leading to the Council of Nicaea, 325, where both Arianism and Sabellianism were excluded.

2. The second and third century Patripassians (Monarchians) Noetus and Praxeas, opposed by Tertullian, taught the absolute unity of God in such a way as to affirm that the Father in the person of Jesus suffered on the cross. Montanus, a second century prophet, claimed to be the incarnation of the Holy Spirit.

3. Apollinaris in the fourth century taught that the word assumed human flesh and biological life (*psuché*) but not a human higher soul or mind. Apollinarianism was condemned in the 370s.

4. Named after Nestorius (381-451) who taught that Mary was not the "mother of God" (*theotokos*), who was born only in human form. Such teaching violated the accepted position that Jesus was as much human as he was divine, even in the womb of Mary.

born of you will be called the son of God" (1:35), that is, my Lord and the Lord of all, Jesus Christ, the only, true Son by nature of God and of Mary, true God and true man.

I believe also that this Son of God and of Mary, our Lord Jesus Christ, suffered for us poor sinners, was crucified, died, and was buried, in order that he might redeem us from sin, death, and the eternal wrath of God by his innocent blood; and that on the third day he arose from the dead, ascended into heaven, and sits at the right hand of God the Father almighty, Lord over all lords, King over all kings and over all created beings in heaven, on earth, and under the earth, over death and life, over sin and righteousness.

Original Sin

For I confess and am able to prove from scripture that all human beings have descended from one man, Adam; and from this man, through their birth, they acquire and inherit the fall, guilt and sin, which the same Adam, through the wickedness of the devil, committed in paradise; and thus all human beings along with him are born, live, and die altogether in sin, and would necessarily be guilty of eternal death if Jesus Christ had not come to our aid and taken upon himself this guilt and sin as an innocent lamb, paid for us by his sufferings, and if he did not still intercede and plead for us as a faithful, merciful Mediator, Savior, and the only Priest and Bishop of our souls.

I herewith reject and condemn as sheer error all doctrines which glorify our free will, as diametrically contrary to the help and grace of our Savior Jesus Christ. Outside of Christ death and sin are our masters and the devil is our god and lord, and there is no power or ability, no cleverness or reason, with which we can prepare ourselves for righteousness and life or seek after it. On the contrary, we must remain the dupes and captives of sin and the property of the devil to do and to think what pleases them and what is contrary to God and his commandments.

Thus I condemn also both the new and the old Pelagians,[5]

---

5. Pelagius, a fifth century heretic opposed especially by Augustine, taught that

who will not admit original sin to be sin, but make it an infirmity or defect. But since death has passed to all people, original sin must be not merely an infirmity but enormous sin, as Paul says, "The wages of sin is death" (1 Cor 15:56). So also David says in Psalm 51:5, "Behold, I was conceived in sin, and in sin did my mother bear me." He does not say, "My mother conceived me with sin," but, "I—I myself—I was conceived in sin, and in sin did my mother bear me," that is, in my mother's womb I have grown from sinful seed, as the Hebrew text signifies. . . .

The holy orders and true religious institutions established by God are these three: the office of priest, the estate of marriage, the civil government. All who are engaged in the clerical office or ministry of the word are in a holy, proper, good, and God-pleasing order and estate, such as those who preach, administer sacraments, supervise the common chest, sextons and messengers or servants who serve such persons. These are engaged in works which are altogether holy in God's sight.

Again, all fathers and mothers who regulate their household wisely and bring up their children to the service of God are engaged in pure holiness, in a holy work and a holy order. Similarly, when children and servants show obedience to their elders and masters, here too is pure holiness, and whoever is thus engaged is a living saint on earth.

Moreover, princes and lords, judges, civil officers, state officials, notaries, male and female servants and all who serve such persons, and further, all their obedient subjects—all are engaged in pure holiness and leading a holy life before God. For these three religious institutions or orders are found in God's word and commandment; and whatever is contained in God's word must be holy, for God's word is holy and sanctifies everything connected with it and involved in it.

Above these three institutions and orders is the common order of Christian love, in which one serves not only the three

---

human salvation was due to the faithful exercise of our free will. Though Pelagianism was condemned at councils in Ephesus, 431, and Orange, 529, subtle versions of this doctrine of self-salvation persistently reappeared.

orders, but also serves every needy person in general with all kinds of benevolent deeds, such as feeding the hungry, giving drink to the thirsty, forgiving enemies, praying for all people on earth, suffering all kinds of evil on earth, etc. Behold, all of these are called good and holy works. However, none of these orders is a means of salvation. There remains only one way above them all, that is, faith in Jesus Christ.

For to be holy and to be saved are two entirely different things. We are saved through Christ alone; but we become holy both through this faith and through these divine foundations and orders. Even the godless may have much about them that is holy without being saved thereby. For God wishes us to perform such works to his praise and glory. And all who are saved in the faith of Christ surely do these works and maintain these orders.

What was said about the estate of marriage, however, should also be applied to widows and unmarried women, for they also belong to the domestic sphere. . . .

God, the Holy Spirit

I believe in the Holy Spirit, who with the Father and the Son is one true God and proceeds eternally from the Father and the Son, yet is a distinct person in the one divine essence and nature. By this Holy Spirit, as a living, eternal, divine gift and endowment, all believers are adorned with faith and other spiritual gifts, raised from the dead, freed from sin, and made joyful and confident, free and secure in their conscience. For this is our assurance, if we feel this witness of the Spirit in our hearts, that God wishes to be our Father, forgive our sin, and bestow everlasting life on us.

These are the three persons and one God, who has given himself to us all wholly and completely, with all that he is and has. The Father gives himself to us, with heaven and earth and all created beings, in order that they may serve us and benefit us. But this gift has become obscured and useless through Adam's fall. Therefore, the Son himself subsequently gave himself and bestowed all his works, sufferings, wisdom, and right-eousness, and reconciled us to the Father, in order that restored to life and righteousness, we might also know and have the Father and his gifts.

But because this grace would benefit no one if it remained so profoundly hidden and could not come to us, the Holy Spirit comes and gives himself to us also, wholly and completely. He teaches us to understand this deed of Christ which has been manifested to us, helps us receive and preserve it, use it to our advantage and impart it to others, increase and extend it. He does this both inwardly and outwardly—inwardly by means of faith and other spiritual gifts, outwardly through the gospel, baptism, and the sacrament of the altar, through which as through three means or methods he comes to us and inculcates the sufferings of Christ for the benefit of our salvation.

Therefore I maintain and know that just as there is no more than one gospel and one Christ, so also there is no more than one baptism. And that baptism in itself is a divine ordinance, as is his gospel also. And just as the gospel is not false or incorrect for the reason that some use it or teach it falsely, or disbelieve it, so also baptism is not false or incorrect even if some have received or administered it without faith, or otherwise misused it. Accordingly, I altogether reject and condemn the teaching of the Anabaptists and Donatists, and all who rebaptize.[6]

In the same way I also say and confess that in the sacrament of the altar the true body and blood of Christ are orally eaten and drunk in the bread and wine, even if the priests who distribute them or those who receive them do not believe, or otherwise misuse the sacrament. It does not rest on human

---

6. Donatists were a rigorist sect in North Africa, originating in the fourth century, who insisted that the holiness of the Church must be judged in terms of the moral purity of its members, and that the ministerial acts of an unholy priest were invalid. Baptism in the orthodox Church therefore was invalid, and converts from that Church had to submit to a true baptism. What the Christian Roman empire thus considered "rebaptism" was made punishable by death in the Code of Justinian, as subversive of Christian society itself, and on that basis the sixteenth century "Anabaptists" were persecuted.

belief or unbelief but on the word and ordinance of God—unless they first change God's word and ordinance and misinterpret them, as the enemies of the sacrament do at the present time. They, indeed, have only bread and wine, for they do not also have the words and instituted ordinance of God but have perverted and changed it according to their own imagination.

One, Holy, Christian Church

I believe that there is one, holy, Christian Church on earth, that is, the community or number or assembly of all Christians in all the world, the one bride of Christ, and his spiritual body of which he is the only head. The bishops or priests are not her heads or lords or bridegrooms, but servants, friends, and—as the word "bishop" implies—superintendents, guardians, or stewards.

This Christian Church exists not only in the realm of the Roman Church or pope, but in all the world, as the prophets foretold that the gospel of Christ would spread throughout the world (Ps 2:8; 19:4). Thus this Christian Church is physically dispersed . . . but spiritually gathered in one gospel and faith, under one head, that is, Jesus Christ. . . .

In this Christian Church, wherever it exists, is to be found the forgiveness of sins, that is, a kingdom of grace and of true pardon. For in it are found the gospel, baptism, and the sacrament of the altar, in which the forgiveness of sins is offered, obtained, and received. Moreover, Christ and his Spirit and God are there. Outside this Christian Church there is no salvation or forgiveness of sins, but everlasting death and damnation; even though there may be a magnificent appearance of holiness and many good works, it is all in vain. But this forgiveness of sins is not to be expected only at one time, as in baptism, as the Novatians teach, but frequently, as often as one needs it, till death.[7]

---

7. Novatian, a third century rigorist, insisted that once baptized, a Christian could not be forgiven a grave sin. Some left-wing Protestants revived this teaching.

For this reason I have a high regard for private confession, for here God's word and absolution are spoken privately and individually to each believer for the forgiveness of one's sins, and as often as one desires it one may have recourse to it for this forgiveness, and also for comfort, counsel, and guidance. Thus it is a precious, useful thing for souls, as long as no one is driven to it with laws and commandments but sinners are left free to make use of it, each according to his or her own need, when and where they wish; just as we are free to obtain counsel and comfort, guidance and instruction when and where our need or our inclination moves us. And as long as one is not forced to enumerate all sins but only those which oppress one most grievously, or those which a person will mention in any case....

Resurrection of the Dead

I believe in the resurrection of all the dead at the last day, both the godly and the wicked, that each may receive in their body their reward according to their merits. Thus the godly will live eternally with Christ and the wicked will perish eternally with the devil and his angels. I do not agree with those who teach that the devils also will finally be restored to salvation.[8]

This is my faith, for so all true Christians believe and so the holy scriptures teach us. On subjects which I have treated too briefly here, my other writings will testify sufficiently, especially those which have been published during the last four or five years. I pray that all godly hearts will bear me witness of this, and pray for me that I may persevere firmly in this faith to the end of my life.

---

8. Origen in the third century taught that the devils would ultimately be converted. Though this view was condemned at Constantinople in 553, it was revived in the sixteenth century.

Catechetical Summary

The best and most popular summary of Luther's faith is contained in the "Small Catechism" of 1529. It was written for the young people to memorize it and to have it explained and discussed with the help of a longer, more detailed "Large Catechism" that appeared shortly before. Both catechisms are based on the traditional model of catechetical handbooks. The medieval catechism consisted of three parts (Decalogue, Creed, Lord's Prayer). Luther added a commentary on baptism and eucharist. Since the laity is called by baptism into a ministry through their vocations, they should know the purpose of the two sacraments which Luther viewed as instituted by the historical Jesus. The "Small Catechism" and the "Augsburg Confession" of 1530 have become the two main normative Lutheran confessions collected in *The Book of Concord* of 1580. The full text of the "Small Catechism" is offered here. (Source: BC, 342-53.)

[I]
The Ten Commandments
in the plain form in which the head of the family
shall teach them to his household

The First

"You shall have no other gods."
What does this mean?
Answer: We should fear and love God, and so we should not use his name to curse, swear, practice magic, lie, or deceive, but in every time of need call upon him, pray to him, praise him, and give him thanks.

The Second

"You shall not take the name of the Lord your God in vain."
What does this mean?

Answer: We should fear and love God, and so we should not use his name to curse, swear, practice magic, lie, or deceive, but in every time of need call upon him, pray to him, praise him, and give him thanks.

The Third

"Remember the Sabbath day,[1] to keep it holy."
What does this mean?
Answer: We should fear and love God, and so we should not despise his word and the preaching of the same, but deem it holy and gladly hear and learn it.

The Fourth

"Honor your father and your mother."
What does this mean?
Answer: We should fear and love God, and so we should not despise our parents and superiors, nor provoke them to anger, but honor, serve, obey, love, and esteem them.

The Fifth

"You shall not kill."
What does this mean?
Answer: We should fear and love God, and so we should not endanger our neighbor's life, nor cause him any harm, but help and befriend him in every necessity of life.

The Sixth

"You shall not commit adultery."
What does this mean?

---

1. Luther's German word *Feiertag* ("holy day and holiday") means day of rest, and this is the original Hebrew meaning of Sabbath, the term employed in the Latin text. The Jewish observance of Saturday is not enjoined here, nor a Sabbatarian observance of Sunday.

Answer: We should fear and love God, and so we should lead a chaste and pure life in word and deed, each one loving and honoring his wife or her husband.

The Seventh

"You shall not steal."
What does this mean?
Answer: We should fear and love God, and so we should not rob our neighbor of his money or property, nor bring them into our possession by dishonest trade or by dealing in shoddy wares, but help him to improve and protect his income and property.

The Eighth

"You shall not bear false witness against your neighbor."
What does this mean?
Answer: We should fear and love God, and so we should not tell lies about our neighbor, nor betray, slander, or defame him, but should apologize for him, speak well of him, and interpret charitably all that he does.

The Ninth

"You shall not covet your neighbor's house."
What does this mean?
Answer: We should fear and love God, and so we should not seek by craftiness to gain possession of our neighbor's inheritance or home, nor to obtain them under pretext of legal right, but be of service and help to him so that he may keep what is his.

The Tenth

"You shall not covet your neighbor's wife, or his manservant, or his maidservant, or his ox, or his ass, or anything that is your neighbor's."

What does this mean?

Answer: We should fear and love God, and so we should not abduct, estrange, or entice away our neighbor's wife, servants, or cattle, but encourage them to remain and discharge their duty to him.

Conclusion

What does God declare concerning all these commandments?

Answer: He says, "I the Lord your God am a jealous God, visiting the iniquity of the fathers upon the children to the third and the fourth generation of those who hate me, but showing steadfast love to thousands of those who love me and keep my commandments."

What does this mean?

Answer: God threatens to punish all who transgress these commandments. We should therefore fear his wrath and not disobey these commandments. On the other hand, he promises grace and every blessing to all who keep them. We should therefore love him, trust in him, and cheerfully do what he has commanded.

[II]
The Creed
in the plain form in which the head of the family
shall teach it to his household

The First Article: Creation

"I believe in God, the Father almighty, maker of heaven and earth."
What does this mean?
Answer: I believe that God has created me and all that exists;
that he has given me and still sustains my body and soul, all my
limbs and senses, my reason and all the faculties of my mind,
together with food and clothing, house and home, family and
property; that he provides me daily and abundantly with all the
necessities of life, protects me from all danger, and preserves
me from all evil. All this he does out of his pure, fatherly, and
divine goodness and mercy, without any merit or worthiness
on my part. For all of this I am bound to thank, praise, serve,
and obey him. This is most certainly true.

The Second Article: Redemption

*"And in Jesus Christ, his only son, our Lord: who was conceived
by the Holy Spirit, born of the Virgin Mary, suffered under Pontius
Pilate, was crucified, died, and was buried: he descended into hell, the
third day he rose from the dead, he ascended into heaven, and is seated
at the right hand of God, the Father almighty, whence he shall come to
judge the living and the dead."*
What does this mean?
Answer: I believe that Jesus Christ, true God, begotten of the
Father from eternity, and also true man, born of the Virgin
Mary, is my Lord, who has redeemed me, a lost and condemned
creature, delivered me and freed me from all sins, from death,
and from the power of the devil, not with silver and gold but
with his holy and precious blood and with his innocent suffer-

ings and death, in order that I may be his, live under him in his kingdom, and serve him in everlasting righteousness, innocence, and blessedness, even as he is risen from the dead and lives and reigns to all eternity. This is most certainly true.

The Third Article: Sanctification

"I believe in the Holy Spirit, the holy Christian Church, the communion of saints, the forgiveness of sins, the resurrection of the body, and the life everlasting. Amen."

What does this mean?

Answer: I believe that by my own reason or strength I cannot believe in Jesus Christ, my Lord, or come to him. But the Holy Spirit has called me through the gospel, enlightened me with his gifts, and sanctified and preserved me in true faith, just as he calls, gathers, enlightens, and sanctifies the whole Christian Church on earth and preserves it in union with Jesus Christ in the one true faith. In this Christian Church he daily and abundantly forgives all my sins, and the sins of all believers, and on the last day he will raise me and all the dead and will grant eternal life to me and to all who believe in Christ. This is most certainly true.

[III]
The Lord's Prayer
in the plain form in which the head of the family
shall teach it to his household

Introduction

"Our Father who art in heaven."

What does this mean?

Answer: Here God would encourage us to believe that he is truly our Father and we are truly his children in order that we may approach him boldly and confidently in prayer, even as beloved children approach their dear father.

The First Petition

"Hallowed be thy name."
What does this mean?
Answer: To be sure, God's name is holy in itself, but we pray in this petition that it may also be holy for us.
How is this done?
Answer: When the word of God is taught clearly and purely and we, as children of God, lead holy lives in accordance with it. Help us to do this, dear Father in heaven! But whoever teaches and lives otherwise than as the word of God teaches, profanes the name of God among us. From this preserve us, heavenly Father!

The Second Petition

"Thy kingdom come."
What does this mean?
Answer: To be sure, the kingdom of God comes of itself, without our prayer, but we pray in this petition that it may also come to us.
How is this done?
Answer: When the heavenly Father gives us his Holy Spirit so that by his grace we may believe his holy word and live a godly life, both here in time and hereafter forever.

The Third Petition

"Thy will be done, on earth as it is in heaven."
What does this mean?
Answer: To be sure, the good and gracious will of God is done without our prayer, but we pray in this petition that it may also be done by us.
How is this done?

Answer: When God curbs and destroys every evil counsel and purpose of the devil, of the world, and of our flesh which would hinder us from hallowing his name and prevent the coming of his kingdom, and when he strengthens us and keeps us steadfast in his word and in faith even to the end. This is his good and gracious will.

The Fourth Petition

"Give us this day our daily bread."
What does this mean?
Answer: To be sure, God provides daily bread, even to the wicked, without our prayer, but we pray in this petition that God may make us aware of his gifts and enable us to receive our daily bread with thanksgiving.
What is meant by daily bread?
Answer: Everything required to satisfy our bodily needs, such as food and clothing, house and home, fields and flocks, money and property; a pious spouse and good children, trustworthy servants, godly and faithful rulers, good government; seasonable weather, peace and health, order and honor; true friends, faithful neighbors, and the like.

The Fifth Petition

"And forgive us our debts, as we also have forgiven our debtors."
What does this mean?
Answer: We pray in this petition that our heavenly Father may not look upon our sins, and on their account deny our prayers, for we neither merit nor deserve those things for which we pray. Although we sin daily and deserve nothing but punishment, we nevertheless pray that God may grant us all things by his grace. And assuredly we on our part will heartily forgive and cheerfully do good to those who may sin against us.

The Sixth Petition

"And lead us not into temptation."
What does this mean?
Answer: God tempts no one to sin, but we pray in this petition that God may so guard and preserve us that the devil, the world, and our flesh may not deceive us or mislead us into unbelief, despair, and other great and shameful sins, but that, although we may be so tempted, we may finally prevail and gain the victory.

The Seventh Petition

"But deliver us from evil."
What does this mean?
Answer: We pray in this petition, as in a summary, that our Father in heaven may deliver us from all manner of evil, whether it affect body or soul, property or reputation, and that at last, when the hour of death comes, he may grant us a blessed end and graciously take us from this world of sorrow to himself in heaven.

Conclusion

"Amen."
What does this mean?
Answer: It means that I should be assured that such petitions are acceptable to our heavenly Father and are heard by him, for he himself commanded us to pray like this and promised to hear us. "Amen, amen" means "Yes, yes, it shall be so."

[IV]
The Sacrament of Holy Baptism
in the plain form in which the head of the family
shall teach it to his household

First

What is baptism?

Answer: Baptism is not merely water, but it is water used according to God's command and connected with God's word.

What is this word of God?

Answer: As recorded in Matthew 28:19, our Lord Christ said, "Go therefore and make disciples of all nations, baptizing them in the name of the Father and of the Son and of the Holy Spirit."

Second

What gifts or benefits does baptism bestow?

Answer: It effects forgiveness of sins, delivers from death and the devil, and grants eternal salvation to all who believe, as the word and promise of God declare.

What is this word and promise of God?

Answer: As recorded in Mark 16:16, our Lord Christ said, "The one who believes and is baptized will be saved; but the one who does not believe will be condemned."

Third

How can water produce such great effects?

Answer: It is not the water that produces these effects, but the word of God connected with the water, and our faith which relies on the word of God it is a baptism, that is, a gracious water of life and a washing of regeneration in the Holy Spirit, as Paul wrote to Titus (3:5-8), "He saved us by the washing of regeneration and renewal in the Holy Spirit, which he poured out upon us richly through Jesus Christ our Savior, so that we might be justified by his grace and become heirs in hope of eternal life. The saying is sure."

Fourth

What does such baptizing with water signify?

Answer: It signifies that the old Adam in us, together with all sins and evil lusts, should be drowned by daily sorrow and repentance and be put to death, and that the new being should come forth daily and rise up, cleansed and righteous, to live forever in God's presence.

Where is this written?

Answer: In Romans 6:4 Paul wrote, "We were buried therefore with him by baptism into death, so that as Christ was raised from the dead by the glory of the Father, we too might walk in newness of life."

[V]
Confession and Absolution
How plain people are to be taught to confess

What is confession?

Answer: Confession consists of two parts. One is that we confess our sins. The other is that we receive absolution or forgiveness from the confessor as from God himself, by no means doubting but firmly believing that our sins are thereby forgiven before God in heaven.

What sins should we confess?

Answer: Before God we should acknowledge that we are guilty of all manner of sins, even those of which we are not aware, as we do in the Lord's Prayer. Before the confessor, however, we should confess only those sins of which we have knowledge and which trouble us.

What are such sins?

Answer: Reflect on your condition in the light of the ten commandments: whether you are a father or mother, a son or daughter, a master or servant; whether you have been disobedient, unfaithful, lazy, ill-tempered, or quarrelsome; whether you have harmed anyone by word or deed; and whether you have stolen, neglected, or wasted anything, or done other evil.

Please give me a brief form of confession.

Answer: You should say to the confessor: "Dear Pastor, please hear my confession and declare that my sins are forgiven for God's sake."

"Proceed."

"I, a poor sinner, confess before God that I am guilty of all sins. In particular I confess in your presence that, as a manservant or maidservant, etc., I am unfaithful to my master, for here and there I have not done what I was told. I have made my master angry, caused him to curse, neglected to do my duty, and caused him to suffer loss. I have also been immodest in word and deed. I have quarreled with my equals. I have grumbled and sworn at my mistress, etc. For all this I am sorry and pray for grace. I mean to do better."

A master or mistress may say: "In particular I confess in your presence that I have not been faithful in training my children, servants, and wife to the glory of God. I have cursed. I have set a bad example by my immodest language and actions. I have injured my neighbors by speaking evil of them, overcharging them, giving them inferior goods and short measure." Masters and mistresses should add whatever else they have done contrary to God's commandments and to their action in life, etc.

If, however, anyone does not feel that his or her conscience is burdened by such or by greater sins, he or she should not worry, nor should he or she search for and invent other sins, for this would turn confession into torture; he or she should simply mention one or two sins of which he is aware. For example, "In particular I confess that I once cursed. On one occasion I also spoke indecently. And I neglected this or that," etc. Let this suffice.

If you have knowledge of no sin at all (which is quite un-likely), you should mention none in particular, but receive forgiveness upon the general confession which you make to God in the presence of the confessor.

Then the confessor shall say: "God be merciful to you and strengthen your faith. Amen."

Again he shall say: "Do you believe that this forgiveness is the forgiveness of God?"

Answer: "Yes, I do."

Then he shall say: "Be it done for you as you have believed (Mt 8:13). According to the command of our Lord Jesus Christ, I forgive you your sins in the name of the Father and of the Son and of the Holy Spirit. Amen. Go in peace (Mk 5:34; Lk 7:50; 8:48)."

A confessor will know additional passages of the scriptures with which to comfort and to strengthen the faith of those whose consciences are heavily burdened or who are distressed and sorely tried. This is intended simply as an ordinary form of confession for plain people.

[VI]
The Sacrament of the Altar
in the plain form in which the head of the family
shall teach it to his household

What is the Sacrament of the Altar?

Answer: Instituted by Christ himself, it is the true body and blood of our Lord Jesus Christ, under the bread and wine, given to us Christians to eat and to drink.

Where is this written?

Answer: The holy evangelists Matthew, Mark, and Luke, and also Paul, write thus: "Our Lord Jesus Christ, on the night when he was betrayed, took bread, and when he had given thanks, he broke it, and gave it to the disciples and said, 'Take, eat; this is my body which is given for you. Do this in remembrance of me.'

In the same way also he took the cup, after supper, and when he had given thanks he gave it to them, saying, 'Drink of it, all of you. This cup is the new covenant in my blood, which is poured out for many for the forgiveness of sins. Do this, as often as you drink it, in remembrance of me.'"[2]

What is the benefit of such eating and drinking?

Answer: We are told in the words "for you" and "for the forgiveness of sins." By these words the forgiveness of sins, life, and salvation are given to us in the sacrament, for where there is forgiveness of sins, there are also life and salvation.

How can bodily eating and drinking produce such great effects?

Answer: The eating and drinking do not in themselves produce them, but the words "for you" and "for the forgiveness of sins." These words, when accompanied by the bodily eating and drinking, are the chief thing in the sacrament, and he who believes these words has what they say and declare: the forgiveness of sins.

Who, then, receives this sacrament worthily?

Answer: Fasting and bodily preparation are a good external discipline, but he is truly worthy and well prepared who believes these words: "for you" and "for the forgiveness of sins." On the other hand, he who does not believe these words, or doubts them, is unworthy and unprepared, for the words "for you" require truly believing hearts.

[VII]
Morning and Evening Prayers
How the head of the family shall teach his household
to say morning and evening prayers

In the morning, when you rise, make the sign of the cross and say, "In the name of God, the Father, the Son, and the Holy Spirit. Amen."

---

2. A conflation of texts from 1 Cor 11:23-25; Mt 26:26-28; Mk 14:22-24; Lk 22:19, 20.

Then, kneeling or standing, say the Apostles' Creed and the Lord's Prayer. Then you may say this prayer:

"I give you thanks, heavenly Father, through your dear Son Jesus Christ, that you have protected me through the night from all harm and danger. I beseech you to keep me this day, too, from all sin and evil, that in all my thoughts, words, and deeds I may please you. Into your hands I commend my body and soul and all that is mine. Let your holy angel have charge of me, that the wicked one may have no power over me. Amen."

After singing a hymn (possibly a hymn on the ten commandments) or whatever your devotion may suggest, you should go to your work joyfully.

In the evening, when you retire, make the sign of the cross and say, "In the name of God, the Father, the Son, and the Holy Spirit. Amen."

Then, kneeling or standing, say the Apostles' Creed and the Lord's Prayer. Then you may say this prayer:

"I give you thanks, heavenly Father, through your dear Son Jesus Christ, that you have this day graciously protected me. I beseech you to forgive all my sins and the wrong which I have done. Graciously protect me during the coming night. Into your hands I commend my body and soul and all that is mine. Let thy holy angels have charge of me, that the wicked one may have no power over me. Amen."

Then quickly lie down and sleep in peace.

Spiritual Formation
and
Pastoral Care

Christ-Centered Living

Luther learned in the monastery the discipline of meditation. It was a form of prayer leading to single-minded service. As monastic rules put it, "pray and work" (*ora et labora*). When Luther was called away from the ordinary life as an Augustinian Hermit, he continued the discipline of meditation in his career as a teacher and priest. He also urged all Christians to meditate, most specifically on what Christ did for them, on his "passion." By 1519 he had composed a treatise entitled "A Meditation on Christ's Passion." It became so popular that it was included in a collection of Luther's sermons for the Church year as the sermon for Good Friday. The collection was used for meditative reading during family devotions, known as "Church postil" (from the Latin for "according to these words of scripture—*post illa verba sacrae scripturae*, the traditional way of starting a sermon in Luther's day). The sermon shows how Luther's piety was still linked to medieval fears of punishment for sin. But Luther also already reflects his spiritual breakthrough to a more joyous, Christ-centered spirituality. The selected text is from the German edition of 1519. (Source: LW 42:7-14.)

Improper Ways

Some people meditate on Christ's passion by venting their anger on the Jews. This singing and ranting about wretched Judas satisfies them, for they are in the habit of complaining about other people, of condemning and reproaching their adversaries. . . .

Some point to the manifold benefits and fruits that grow from contemplating Christ's passion. There is a saying ascribed to Albertus[1] about this, that it is more beneficial to ponder Christ's passion just once than to fast a whole year or to pray a psalm daily, etc. These people follow this saying blindly and therefore do not reap the fruit of Christ's passion, for in so doing they are seeking their own advantage. They carry pictures and booklets, letters and crosses on their person. Some who travel afar do this

---

1. Albert Magnus (1193-1280) was a scholastic theologian and a teacher of Thomas Aquinas.

141

in the belief that they thus protect themselves against water and sword, fire, and all sorts of perils. Christ's suffering is thus used to effect in them a lack of suffering contrary to his being and nature.

Some feel pity for Christ, lamenting and bewailing his innocence. They are like the women who followed Christ from Jerusalem and were chided and told by Christ that it would be better to weep for themselves and their children (Lk 23:27-28). They are the kind of people who go far afield in their meditation on the passion, making much of Christ's farewell from Bethany (Jn 12:1-8) and of the Virgin Mary's anguish (Jn 19:25-27), but never progressing beyond that, which is why so many hours are devoted to the contemplation of Christ's passion.

Also to this group belong those who have learned what rich fruits the holy Mass offers. In their simplemindedness they think it enough simply to hear Mass . . . that it is effective in itself without our merit and worthiness, and that this is all that is needed. Yet, the Mass was not instituted for its own worthiness, but to make us worthy and to remind us of the passion of Christ. Where that is not done, we make of the Mass a physical and unfruitful act, though even this is of some good. Of what help is it to you that God is God, if he is not God to you? Of what benefit is it to you that food and drink are good and wholesome in themselves if they are not healthful for you? And it is to be feared that many Masses will not improve matters as long as we do not seek the right fruit in them.

Proper Ways

They contemplate Christ's passion aright who view it with a terror-stricken heart and a despairing conscience. This terror must be felt as you witness the stern wrath and the unchanging earnestness with which God looks upon sin and sinners, so much so that he was unwilling to release sinners even for his only and dearest Son without his payment of the severest penalty for them. Thus he says in Isaiah 53:8, "I have chastised him for the transgressions of my people." If the dearest child is punished thus, what will be the fate of sinners? (Lk 23:31). It must be an inexpressible and unbearable earnestness that forces such a great and infinite person to suffer and die to appease it. And if you seriously consider that it is God's very own Son, the eternal wisdom of the Father, who suffers, you will be terrified indeed. The more you think about it, the more intensely will you be frightened. . . .

The main benefit of Christ's passion is that we see into our own true self and that we be terrified and crushed by this. Unless we seek that knowledge, we do not derive much benefit from Christ's passion. The real and true work of Christ's passion is to make us conformable to Christ, so that our conscience is tormented by our sins in like measure as Christ was pitiably tormented in body and soul by our sins. This does not call for many words but for profound reflection and a great awe of sins. Take this as an illustration: A criminal is sentenced to death for the murder of the child of a prince or a king. In the meantime you go your carefree way, singing and playing, until you are cruelly arrested and convicted of having inspired the murderer. Now the whole world closes in upon you, especially since your conscience also deserts you. You should be terrified even more by the meditation on Christ's passion. For the evildoers whom God has judged and driven out, were only the servants of your sin; you are actually the one who, as we said, sinning killed and crucified God's Son.

Who is so hardhearted and callous as not to be terrified by Christ's passion and led to a knowledge of self, has reason to fear. For it is inevitable, whether in this life or in hell, that you will have to become conformable to Christ's image and suffering. At the very least, you will sink into this terror in the hour of death and will tremble and quake and feel all that Christ suffered on the cross. Since it is horrible to lie waiting on your deathbed, you should pray God to soften your heart and let you now ponder Christ's passion. No meditation or any other doctrine is granted to you that you might be boldly inspired by your own will to accomplish this. You must first seek God's grace and ask that it be accomplished by his grace and not by your own power. That is why the people we referred to above fail to view Christ's passion aright. They do not seek God's help for this, but look to their own ability to devise their own means of accomplishing this. They deal with the matter in a completely human but also unfruitful way.

We say without hesitation that who contemplates God's sufferings for a day, an hour, yes, only a quarter of an hour, does better than to fast a whole year, pray a psalm daily, yes, better than to hear a hundred Masses. This meditation changes our being and, almost like baptism, gives us a new birth. Here the passion of Christ performs its natural and noble work, strangling the old Adam and banishing all joy, delight, and confidence which we could derive from other created beings, even as Christ was forsaken by all, even by God.

Since this [strangling of the old Adam] does not rest with us, it happens that we occasionally pray for it, and yet do not attain it at once. Nevertheless we should neither despair nor desist. At times this happens because we do not pray for it as God conceives of it and wishes it, for it must be left free and unfettered. Then we become sad in our conscience and grumble to ourselves about the evil in our life. It may well be that we do not know that Christ's passion, to which we give no thought, is effecting this in us, even as the others who do think of Christ's passion still do not gain this knowledge of self through it. For these the passion of Christ is hidden and genuine, while for those it is only unreal and misleading. In that way God often reverses matters, so that those who do not meditate on Christ's passion do meditate on it, and those who do not hear Mass do hear it, and those who hear it do not hear it. . . .

After we have thus become aware of our sin and are terrified in our heart, we must watch that sin does not remain in our conscience, for this would lead to sheer despair. Just as [our knowledge of] sin flowed from Christ and was acknowledged by us, so we must pour this sin back on him and free our conscience of it. Therefore beware, lest you do as those perverse people who torture their hearts with their sins and strive to do the impossible, namely, get rid of their sins by running from one good work or penance to another. . . . .

You cast your sins from yourself and onto Christ when you firmly believe that his wounds and sufferings are your sins, to be borne and paid for by him, as we read in Isaiah 53:6, "The Lord has laid on him the iniquity of us all." Peter says, "in his body has he borne our sins on the wood of the cross" (1 Pt 2:24). Paul says, "God has made him a sinner for us, so that through him we would be made just" (2 Cor 5:21). You must stake everything on these and similar verses. The more your conscience torments you, the more tenaciously must you cling to them. If you do not do that, but presume to still your conscience with your contrition and penance, you will never obtain peace of mind, but will have to despair in the end. If we allow sin to remain in our conscience and try to deal with it there, or if we look at sin in our heart, it will be much too strong for us and will live on forever. But if we behold it resting on Christ and [see it] overcome by his resurrection, and then boldly believe this, it is dead and nullified. Sin cannot remain on Christ, since it is swallowed up by his resurrection. Now you see no wounds, no pain in him, and no sign of sin. Thus Paul declared that "Christ died for our sins and rose for our justification" (Rom 4:25). That is to say, in his suffering Christ makes our sin known and thus destroys it, but through his resurrection he justifies us and delivers us from all sin, if we believe this.

If, as was said before, you cannot believe, you must entreat God for faith. This too rests entirely in the hands of God. What we said about suffering also applies here, namely, that sometimes faith is granted openly, sometimes in secret.

However, you can spur yourself on to believe. First of all, you must no longer contemplate the suffering of Christ (for this has already done its work and terrified you), but pass beyond that and see his friendly heart and how this heart beats with such love for you that it impels him to bear with pain your conscience and your sin. Then your heart will be filled with love for him, and the confidence of your faith will be strengthened. Now continue and rise beyond Christ's heart to God's heart and you will see that Christ would not have shown this love for you if God in his eternal love had not wanted this, for Christ's love for you is due to his obedience to God. Thus you will find the divine and kind paternal heart, and, as Christ says, you will be drawn to the Father through him. Then you will understand the words of Christ, "For God so loved the world that he gave his only Son" (Jn 3:16). We know God aright when we grasp him not in his might or wisdom (for then he proves terrifying), but in his kindness and love. Then faith and confidence are able to exist, and then we are truly born anew in God.

After your heart has thus become firm in Christ, and love, not fear of pain, has made you a foe of sin, then Christ's passion must from that day on become a pattern for your entire life. Henceforth you will have to see his passion differently. Until now we regarded it as a sacrament which is active in us while we are passive, but now we find that we too must be active, namely, in the following. If pain or sickness afflicts you, consider how paltry this is in comparison with the thorny crown and the nails of Christ. If you are obliged to do or to refrain from doing things against your wishes, ponder how Christ was bound and captured and led hither and yon. If you are beset by pride, see how your Lord was mocked and ridiculed along with criminals. If unchastity and lust assail you, remember how ruthlessly Christ's tender flesh was scourged, pierced, and beaten. If hatred, envy, and vindictiveness beset you, recall that Christ, who indeed had more reason to avenge himself, interceded with tears and cries for you and for all his enemies. If sadness or any adversity, physical or spiritual, distresses you, strengthen your heart and say, "Well, why should I not be willing to bear a little grief, when agonies and fears caused my Lord to sweat blood in the Garden of Gethsemane? He who lies abed while his master struggles in the throes of death is indeed a slothful and disgraceful servant."

So then, this is how we can draw strength and encouragement from Christ against every vice and failing. That is a proper contemplation of Christ's passion, and such are its fruits. And he who exercises himself in that way does better than to listen to every story of Christ's passion or to read all the Masses. This is not to say that Masses are of no value, but they do not help us in such meditation and exercise. Those who thus make Christ's life and name a part of their own lives are true Christians. Paul says, "Those who belong to Christ have crucified their flesh with all its desires" (Gal 5:24). Christ's passion must be met not with words or forms, but with life and truth. Thus Paul exhorts us, "Consider him who endured such hostility from evil people against himself, so that you may be strengthened and not be weary at heart" (Heb 12:3). And Peter, "Since therefore Christ suffered in the flesh, strengthen and arm yourselves by meditating on this" (1 Pt 4:1).

Baptism

Baptism is the sacrament of Christian unity. It initiates into discipleship with Christ, into the Church. Luther lifted up the fundamental significance of baptism as the source for spiritual formation. He described the meaning and effect of baptism in 1519 in the treatise "The Holy and Blessed Sacrament of Baptism." It was intended to be a simple and logical interpretation of baptism; it appeared in numerous German and Latin editions in various German cities. This selection is from the first edition in 1519. (Source: LW 35:29-43.)

Baptism is *baptismos* in Greek, and *mersio* in Latin, and means to plunge something completely into the water, so that the water covers it. Although in many places it is no longer customary to thrust and dip infants into the font, but only with the hand to pour the baptismal water upon them out of the font, nevertheless the former is what should be done. It would be proper, according to the meaning of the German word *Taufe*, that the infant, or whoever is to be baptized, should be put in and sunk completely into the water and then drawn out again. For even in the German tongue the word *Taufe* comes undoubtedly from the word *tief* [deep] and means that what is baptized is sunk deeply into the water. This usage is also demanded by the significance of baptism itself. For baptism, as we shall hear, signifies that the old self and the sinful birth of flesh and blood are to be wholly drowned by the grace of God. We should therefore do justice to its meaning and make baptism a true and complete sign of the thing it signifies.

Baptism is an external sign or token, which so separates us from all those that are not baptized that we are thereby known as a people of Christ, our leader, under whose banner of the holy cross we continually fight against sin. In this holy sacrament we must therefore pay attention to three things: the sign, the significance of it, and the faith.

A Sign

The sign consists in this, that we are thrust into the water in the name of the Father and of the Son and of the Holy Spirit; however, we are not left there but are drawn out again. . . . The sign must thus have both its parts, the putting in and the drawing out.

The significance of baptism is a blessed dying unto sin and a resurrection in the grace of God, so that the old self, conceived and born in sin, is there drowned, and a new self, born in grace, comes forth and rises. Thus Paul, in Titus 3:5, calls baptism a "washing of regeneration," since in this washing a person is born again and made new. As Christ also says, in John 3:3, 5, "Unless you are born again of water and the Spirit (of grace), you may not enter into the kingdom of heaven." For just as a child is drawn out of his mother's womb and is born, and through this fleshly birth is a sinful person and a child of wrath (Eph 2:3), so one is drawn out of baptism and is born spiritually. This spiritual birth produces a child of grace and a justified person. Therefore sins are drowned in baptism, and in place of sin, righteousness comes forth.

This significance of baptism—the dying or drowning of sin—is not fulfilled completely in this life. Indeed this does not happen until the person passes through bodily death and completely decays to dust. As we can plainly see, the sacrament or sign of baptism is quickly over. But the spiritual baptism, the drowning of sin, which it signifies, lasts as long as we live and is completed only in death. Then it is that a person is completely sunk in baptism, and that which baptism signifies comes to pass. . . .

Similarly, the lifting up out of the baptismal water is quickly done, but the thing it signifies—the spiritual birth and the increase of grace and righteousness—even though it begins in baptism, lasts until death, indeed, until the last day. Only then will that be finished which the lifting up out of baptism signifies. Then shall we arise from death, from sins, and from all evil, pure in body and soul, and then shall we live eternally. Then shall we be truly lifted up out of baptism and be completely born, and we shall put on the true baptismal garment of immortal life in heaven. It is as if the sponsors, when they lift the child up out of baptism, were to say, "Lo your sins are now drowned, and we receive you in God's name into an eternal life of innocence." For in this way will the angels at the last day raise up all Christians—all the devout baptized—and will there fulfill what baptism and the sponsors signify, as Christ declares in Matthew 24:31, "He will send out his angels, and they will gather unto him his elect from the four places of the winds, from the rising to the setting of the sun."

Baptism was foreshown of old in Noah's flood, when the whole world was drowned, except for Noah with his three sons and their wives, eight souls, who were saved in the ark. That the people of the world were drowned signifies that in baptism sins are drowned. But that the eight in the ark, with animals of every sort, were preserved, signifies—as Peter explains in his second epistle (Pt 2:5; cf. Pt 3:20-21)—that through baptism we are saved. Now baptism is by far a greater flood than was that of Noah. For that flood drowned people during no more than one year, but baptism drowns all sorts of people throughout the world, from the birth of Christ even till the day of judgment. Moreover while that was a flood of wrath, this is a flood of grace, as is declared in Psalm 29:10. For without doubt many more people have been baptized than were drowned in the flood.

Its Effect

From this it follows, to be sure, that when someone comes forth out of baptism, he or she is truly pure, without sin, and wholly guiltless. Still, there are many who do not properly understand this. They think that sin is no longer present, and so they become remiss and negligent in the killing of their sinful nature, even as some do when they have gone to confession. For this reason, as I have said above, it should be properly understood and known that our flesh, so long as it lives here, is by nature wicked and sinful.

To correct this wickedness God has devised the plan of making our flesh altogether new, even as Jeremiah shows (18:4-6). For the potter, when the vessel "was spoiled in his hand," thrust it again into the lump of clay and kneaded it, and afterward made another vessel, as seemed good to him. "So," says God, "are you in my hands." In the first birth we are spoiled; therefore he thrusts us into the earth again by death, and makes us over at the last day, that we may be perfect and without sin.

This plan, as has been said, begins in baptism, which signifies death and the resurrection at the last day. Therefore so far as the sign of the sacrament and its significance are concerned, sins and the person are both already dead, and we have risen again; and so the sacrament has taken place. But the work of the sacrament has not yet been fully done, which is to say that death and the resurrection at the last day are still before us. . . .

You ask, "How does baptism help me, if it does not altogether blot out and remove sin?" This is the place for a right understanding of the sacrament of baptism. This blessed sacrament of baptism helps you because in it God allies himself with you and becomes one with you in a gracious covenant of comfort.

In the first place you give yourself up to the sacrament of baptism and to what it signifies. That is, you desire to die, together with your sins, and to be made new at the last day. This is what the sacrament declares, as has been said. God accepts this desire at your hands and grants you baptism. From that hour he begins to make you a new person. He pours into you his grace and Holy Spirit, who begins to slay nature and sin, and to prepare you for death and the resurrection at the last day.

In the second place you pledge yourself to continue in this desire, and to slay your sin more and more as long as you live, even until your dying day. This too God accepts. He trains and tests you all your life long, with many good works and with all kinds of sufferings. Thereby he accomplishes what you in baptism have desired, namely, that you may become free from sin, die, and rise again at the last day, and so fulfill your baptism. . . .

Now if this covenant did not exist, and God were not so

merciful as to wink at our sins, there could be no sin so small but it would condemn us. For the judgment of God can endure no sin. Therefore there is no greater comfort on earth than baptism. For it is through baptism that we come under the judgment of grace and mercy, which does not condemn our sins but drives them out by many trials. . . .

Faith

Here, then, is the place to discuss the third thing in the sacrament: faith. Faith means that one firmly believes all this: that this sacrament not only signifies death and the resurrection at the last day, by which a person is made new to live without sin eternally, but also that it assuredly begins and achieves this; that it establishes a covenant between us and God to the effect that we will fight against sin and slay it, even to our dying breath, while he for his part will be merciful to us, deal graciously with us, and—because we are not sinless in this life until purified by death—not judge us with severity.

So you understand how in baptism a person becomes guiltless, pure, and sinless, while at the same time continuing full of evil inclinations. We can be called pure only in the sense that we have started to become pure and have a sign and covenant of this purity and are ever to become more pure. Because of this God will not count against us our former impurity. A person is thus pure by the gracious imputation of God, rather than by virtue of his or her own nature. As the prophet says in Psalm 32:1-2, "Blessed is the one whose transgression is forgiven; blessed is the one to whom the Lord imputes no iniquity."

This faith is of all things the most necessary, for it is the ground of all comfort. Who does not possess such faith must despair of his or her sins. For the sin which remains after baptism makes it impossible for any good works to be pure before God. For this reason we must boldly and without fear hold fast to our baptism, and set it high against all sins and terrors of conscience. We must humbly admit, "I know full well that I cannot do a single thing that is pure. But I am baptized, and through my baptism God, who cannot lie, has bound himself in a covenant with me. He will not count my sin against me, but will slay it and blot it out."

So, then, we understand that the innocence which is ours by baptism is so called simply and solely because of the mercy of God. For he has begun this work in us, he bears patiently with our sin, and he regards us as if we were sinless. . . . It is because through baptism they have begun to become pure; by God's mercy, with respect to the sins that still remain, they are not condemned; until, finally, through death and at the last day, they become wholly pure, just as the sign of baptism shows.

Therefore those people err greatly who think that through baptism they have become wholly pure. They go about in their ignorance and do not slay their sin. Indeed they do not admit that it is sin. They simply persist in it, and so make their baptism of no effect. They continue to depend only on a few external works. Meanwhile pride, hatred, and other evils in their nature, which they disregard, grow worse and worse.

To speak quite plainly, it is one thing to forgive sins, and another thing to put them away or drive them out. The forgiveness of sins is obtained by faith, even though they are not entirely driven out. But to drive out sins is to exercise ourselves against them, and at last it is to die, for in death sin perishes completely. But both the forgiveness and the driving out of sins are the work of baptism. Thus the apostle writes to the Hebrews, who were baptized and whose sins were forgiven, that they should lay aside the sin which clings to them (12:1). For so long as I believe that God will not count my sins against me, my baptism is in force and my sins are forgiven, even though they may still in a great measure be present. After that follows their driving out through sufferings, death, and the like. This is what we confess in the article [of the Creed], "I believe in the Holy Ghost, the forgiveness of sins," and so forth. Here there is special reference to baptism, in which the forgiveness takes place through God's covenant with us; therefore we must not doubt this forgiveness.

Baptismal Discipline

It follows, then, that baptism makes all sufferings, and especially death, profitable and helpful, so that they simply have to serve baptism in the doing of its work, that is, in the slaying of sin. It cannot be otherwise. For who would fulfill the work and purpose of his baptism and be rid of sin, must die. Sin, however, does not like to die, and for this reason it makes death so bitter and so horrible. Such is the grace and power of God that sin, which has brought death, is driven out again by its very own work, namely, by death itself.

You find many people who wish to live in order that they may become righteous and who say that they would like to be righteous. Now there is no shorter way or manner than through baptism and the work of baptism, which is suffering and death. Yet so long as they are not willing to take this way, it is a sign that they do not properly intend or know how to become righteous. Therefore, God has instituted many estates in life in which people are to learn to exercise themselves and to suffer. To some he has commanded the estate of matrimony, to others the estate of the clergy, to others the estate of temporal rule, and to all he has commanded that they shall toil and labor to kill the flesh and accustom it to death. Because for all who are baptized, their baptism has made the repose, ease, and prosperity of this life a very poison and a hindrance to its work. For in the easy life no one learns to suffer, to die with gladness, to get rid of sin, and to live in harmony with baptism. Instead there grows only love of this life and horror of eternal life, fear of death and unwillingness to blot out sin.

Consider now the lives of people. Many there are who fast, pray, go on pilgrimage, and exercise themselves in such things, thinking thereby only to heap up merit and to sit down in the high places of heaven; they no longer learn to slay their evil vices. But fasting and all such exercises should be aimed at holding down the old Adam, the sinful nature, and at accustoming it to do without all that is pleasing for this life, and thus preparing it more and more each day for death, so that the work and purpose of baptism may be fulfilled. And all these exercises and toils are to be measured not by their number or their greatness, but by the demands of baptism. That is to say, we are to take upon ourselves so much of these works as is good and profitable for the suppressing of our sinful nature and for the preparation of it for death. We are to increase or diminish these works according as we see sin increasing or diminishing. . . .

God has given every saint a special way and a special grace for living according to his or her baptism. But baptism and its significance God has set as a common standard for everyone. We are to examine ourselves according to our station in life and are to find what is the best way for us to fulfill the work and purpose of our baptism, namely, to slay sin and to die in order that Christ's burden may thus grow light and easy (Mt 11:30) and not be carried with worry and care. Solomon has this to say of it, "The toil of fools wears them out, because they don't know the way to the city" (Eccl 10:15). For even as they are worried who wish to go to the city and cannot find their way, so it is with us also; all our life and labor is a burden to them, and yet accomplishes nothing. . . .

In truth, those who do not see in God's grace how it bears with them as sinners and will make them blessed, those who look forward only to God's judgment, will never be joyful in God, and can neither love nor praise him. But if we hear and firmly believe that in the covenant of baptism God receives us sinners, spares us, and makes us pure from day to day, then our heart must be joyful, and love and praise God. Thus God says through the prophet, "I will spare them as a man spares his son" (Mal 3:17). Wherefore it is needful that we give thanks to the blessed Majesty, who shows himself so gracious and merciful toward us poor condemned worms.

Eucharist

There has been an enduring discussion in Christian history concerning the proper reception of the eucharist. Increasing emphasis was put on a "worthy" reception of Christ in the Mass during the Middle Ages. "Worthy" came to mean moral purity rather the desire to find comfort and forgiveness for a terrified conscience (as Luther experienced it). That is why Luther preached on the topic of worthy reception on Holy Thursday of 1521, entitled "A Sermon on the Worthy Reception of the Sacrament." It focused on the reception by penitent sinners rather than by those who felt morally worthy to receive the eucharist. The selection is based on the German text of the first edition. (Source: LW 42:171-77.)

Conditions

Those who openly live in sin or who wilfully harbor evil thoughts, such as of hatred, of uncleanness, and the like, shall not receive the sacrament. Until they shun these sins, the Church's precept is not meant for them. It is better to obey God's command than that of the Church (Acts 5:29). It is better to refrain from receiving the sacrament than to receive it and thereby sin against God's commandment, which forbids the holy sacrament to such sinners.[1]

Those who find that they are prompted to partake of it merely because of the order of the Church or from habit, who, if wholly free to choose, would not come to it with good will and longing, also must not partake of the sacrament. As Augustine says, the sacrament seeks a hungry, thirsty, and desirous soul which yearns for it. But those who go only because of command or out of habit feel no desire or longing for it, but rather horror or dread, so that they would rather be away from it than near it. Persons with a yearning heart do not wait for a command, nor are they moved by precept or habit. Such persons are driven by

---

1. The "commandment" Luther had in mind may be 1 Cor 11:28-29.

their need and their desire. They have their mind fixed only on the sacrament, which they desire.

You may say that if this is true, then there is reason to fear that only a few people in the world receive the sacrament worthily, since almost everybody receives it not by free choice but only in obedience to the Church. My answer is that this does not alter the facts. There must be hunger and thirst for this food and drink; otherwise harm is sure to follow. The same is true in nature. When your body is sated and filled, and yet you partake of a plentiful and rich meal, this is bound to end in sickness and death. But if your body is hungry and thirsty, such a meal will make you cheerful, healthy, and strong. . . .

Such hunger and thirst are created not by compelling people, but by showing them their frailty and their need so that they will see their wretched condition and feel the desire to be delivered from it. This happens, for instance, when you recognize that you are weak in faith, cold in love, and faint in hope. You will find that you are disposed toward hatred and impatience, impurity, greed, and whatever other vice there is. This you will undoubtedly find and feel if you really look at yourself. All the saints have found this to be true about themselves. You must also see whether you have weakly yielded or would have fallen prey to one or the other. To know and understand your sin and to be willing to resolve to get rid of such vice and evil and to long to become pure, modest, gentle, mild, humble, believing, loving, etc.—that is the beginning of such hunger and thirst.

The greater and more fervent this desire is in you, the better fit you are to receive the sacrament. God has given his commandment so that you might thereby know your sin. . . .

When we have this hunger and so are prepared for the sacrament, we must carefully avoid receiving it while trusting in our own worthiness. Nor must we merely pray, as some do, "Lord, I am not worthy to have you come under my roof; but say only a word, and my soul will be healed" (Mt 8:8). I am not rejecting that prayer, but one should be aware of something else.

I am referring to the words Christ spoke when he instituted the Mass: "Take, eat, this is my body which is given for you. Take, drink, all of you; for it is the cup of the new and eternal testament in my blood, poured out for you and for all for the forgiveness of sins" (Mt 26:26-28). . . .

All Christians should have these words close to themselves and put their minds on them above all others. For just as they are meant for us all, so they are spoken by the priest in the stead of Christ to all who stand around him. We should take all of these words to heart, placing our trust in them and not doubting that with these the Lord invites us to be his guests at this abundant meal.

The priest's elevation of the sacrament and the cup, together with the ringing of the bells, has no other purpose than to remind us of the words of Christ. It is as if the priest and the bell-ringer were saying to us all, "Listen, you Christians, and see, take and eat, take and drink, etc. 'This is the body and this is the blood of Christ,' spoken softly by the priest, but heard clearly and audibly by us. With these words you must now edify your hungry heart and rely upon the truth of this divine promise, then receive the sacrament, make your way to God, and say, 'Lord, it is true that I am not worthy for you to come under my roof, but I need and desire your help and grace to make me godly. I now come to you, trusting only in the wonderful words I just heard, with which you invite me to your table and promise me, the unworthy one, forgiveness of all my sins through your body and blood if I eat and drink them in this sacrament. Amen. Dear Lord, I do not doubt the truth of your words. Trusting them, I eat and I drink with you. Do unto me according to your words. Amen.' "

Worthy reception of the sacrament, however, is not based on our diligence and effort, our work and prayers, or our fasting, but on the truth of the divine words. To be sure, some invented various fruits of the Mass to stimulate a desire and longing for the sacrament. One devised this fruit, another that. Some among them write that who comes to the Mass will not grow older.

They have fooled with it so long that they have made the fruits of the Mass appear to be nothing but bodily and temporal benefits, although they have no authority beyond their own dreams to do this. They also believe that the Mass assures security and happiness for the day on which it is heard. Nothing has remained of the Mass, that is, of the meaning and use of this divine promise, which is really the whole essence of the Mass. For during the Last Supper the Lord instituted only these words, and he gave them to us solely for spiritual purposes, such as the remission of sin and the reception of grace and help so that the human heart, clinging to these words by faith, should gain strength in everything good against sin, death, and hell. His word and work were not intended to help us in a temporal way, but in a spiritual and eternal way. It is an insult to God to misuse these for the attainment of temporal benefits.

Administration

When the pastor administers the sacrament, it must be understood that he is acting in accord with Christ's words, "Take, and eat," etc. We should receive the sacrament on the strength of these words, be mindful of them, and not doubt that in us there takes place the intent and content of those same words of Christ, namely, that Christ's body is given for us and that his blood was shed for us, and that we are heirs of the New Testament, that is, of God's grace and favor for eternal life. Faith creates godliness and drives out all sin, grants strength in sickness, enlightens in all blindness, heals all evil inclinations, guards against sin, and performs every good deed. In brief, the fruit of such faith is that never can there remain any frailty; for in faith the Holy Spirit is given, and thereby a person loves God because of the abundant goodness received from him. A person becomes cheerful and glad to do all that is good without the compulsion of law and command.

Just see how far those who taught us that if we wanted to receive the sacrament worthily we would have to be perfectly pure have departed from the proper path. They made us shy and timid. They reduced the sweet and blessed sacrament to a frightful and hazardous act. As a result, only a few people come to the sacrament with joy and longing, since they constantly fear that they are not pure and worthy enough. It is just this worry and fear that makes them unworthy and, at the same time, drives out hunger and thirst. Fear and desire cannot exist side by side. Thus they hindered us with the very means by which they thought to advance us. If you do not want to come to the sacrament until you are perfectly clean and whole, it would be better for you to remain away entirely. The sacrament is to purify you and help you. Yet you do not want to come until you no longer need its help and have already helped yourself. This is just as if you were invited to a splendid banquet and would gorge and swill before you went. Then, as you sit at table, you would feel nauseated and miserable, while all the fine dishes would be served you in vain. How would your host like that?

You see, that is what happens when one tries to make people pious and lead them to the right by means of commandments and laws. It only makes them worse. Thanks to such tactics, they do unwillingly and drearily whatever they do. This becomes a hindrance to God's grace and sacrament. God neither wants to nor will he grant this grace to those who were forced, pressed, and driven to the sacrament by commandment and law, but only to hearts that long and pine and thirst for it, to hearts that come voluntarily. In Matthew 11:12 Christ says, "Since the days of John the Baptist the kingdom of heaven has suffered violence, and men of violence took it by force." That is to say: Since John showed the people their sins and shortcomings, which all pastors should do, they longed so for the kingdom of God and its help that they immediately and forcefully pressed toward it and seized it. God loves such guests; they who are thus hounded by their sins and transgressions are welcome to him. Psalm 42:1 reads, "As a hunted hart longs for a fountain of fresh water, so my soul longs for you, O God."

Purpose

Christ entices us similarly in Matthew 11:28, saying, "Come to me, all you who labor and are heavy-laden, and I will refresh and help you." It is out of the question that the Lord is here speaking about physical labor or burdens, for he helps only the soul. Therefore, these words of his must be understood to refer to the labor and the burden of the conscience, which is nothing else than a bad conscience oppressed by sins committed, by daily transgressions, and by a yearning toward sin. The Lord does not drive all such people from him, as do those who teach that we must come to the sacrament with purity and worthiness. Nor does he issue a command or compel anyone to go to the sacrament, but rather he kindly invites and encourages all who are sinners and find themselves burdened and who yearn for help. The sublime sacrament must be regarded by us not as a poison, but as a medicine for the soul. Christ himself declares in Matthew 9:12, "Those who are well have no need of a physician, but those who are sick." The only question is whether you thoroughly recognize and feel your labor and your burden and that you yourself fervently desire to be relieved of these. Then you are indeed worthy of the sacrament. If you believe, the sacrament gives you everything you need.

The Plague

The bubonic plague or "black death" was Europe's curse from 1347 until 1350. Various epidemics struck Germany in the fifteenth and sixteenth centuries, including Wittenberg in the summer of 1527. Spread by infected rats, fleas, and other vermin, the disease caused fever, made the lymph glands swell, and was highly contagious. The mortality rate was often ninety per cent. When the plague struck Wittenberg the university closed. Luther stayed, visiting many dying parishioners. Should Christians flee or stay to serve the neighbor in need? Luther dealt with the question asked by a pastor in a pamphlet, *Whether One May Flee From a Deadly Plague,* 1527. Luther may give the impression that the plague was a punishment from God. This was a prevailing medieval view. But Luther transcends this view by advocating realistic care for the victims through medicine and prayer. (Source: LW 43:119-38.)

Public Duty

To begin with, some people are of the firm opinion that one need not and should not run away from a deadly plague. Rather, since death is God's punishment, which he sends upon us for our sins, we must submit to God and with a true and firm faith patiently await our punishment. They look upon running away as an outright wrong and as lack of belief in God. Others take the position that one may properly flee, particularly if one holds no public office.

I cannot censure the former for their excellent decision. They uphold a good cause, namely, a strong faith in God, and deserve commendation because they desire every Christian to hold to a strong, firm faith. It takes more than a milk faith to await a death before which most of the saints themselves have been and still are in dread (cf. 1 Cor 3:2). Who would not acclaim these earnest people to whom death is a little thing? They willingly accept God's chastisement, doing so without tempting God, as we shall hear later on.

Since it is generally true of Christians that few are strong and many are weak, one simply cannot place the same burden upon everyone. A person who has a strong faith can drink poison and suffer no harm, Mark 16:18, while one who has a weak faith would thereby drink to his death. Peter could walk upon the water because he was strong in faith. When he began to doubt and his faith weakened, he sank and almost drowned (cf. Mt 14:30). When a strong man travels with a weak one, he must restrain himself so as not to walk at a speed proportionate to his strength lest he set a killing pace for his weak companion. Christ does not want his weak ones to be abandoned, as Paul teaches in Romans 15:1 and 1 Corinthians 12:22ff. To put it briefly and concisely, running away from death may happen in one of two ways. First, it may happen in disobedience to God's word and command. For instance, in the case of a man who is imprisoned for the sake of God's word. In such a situation everyone has Christ's plain mandate and command not to flee but rather to suffer death, as he says, "Whoever denies me before men, I will also deny before my Father who is in heaven" and "Do not fear those who kill the body but cannot kill the soul" (Mt 10:28, 33).

Those who are engaged in a spiritual ministry such as preachers and pastors must likewise remain steadfast before the peril of death. We have a plain command from Christ, "A good shepherd lays down his life for the sheep but the hireling sees the wolf coming and flees" (Jn 10:11). For when people are dying, they most need a spiritual ministry which strengthens and comforts their consciences by word and sacrament and in faith overcomes death. However, where enough preachers are available in one locality and they agree to encourage the other clergy to leave in order not to expose themselves needlessly to danger, I do not consider such conduct sinful because spiritual services are provided for and because they would have been ready and willing to stay if it had been necessary. We read that St. Athanasius fled from his Church that his life might be spared because many others were there to administer his office. Similarly, the brethren in Damascus lowered Paul in a basket over the wall to make it possible for him to escape (Acts 9:25). And also in Acts 19:30 Paul allowed himself to be kept from risking danger in the marketplace, because it was not essential for him to do so.

Accordingly, all those in public office such as mayors, judges, and the like are under obligation to remain. This, too, is God's word, which institutes secular authority and commands that town and country be ruled, protected, and preserved, as Paul teaches in Romans 13:4, "The governing authorities are God's ministers for your own good." To abandon an entire community which one has been called to govern and to leave it without official or government, exposed to all kinds of danger such as fires, murder, riots, and every imaginable disaster is a great sin. It is the kind of disaster the devil would like to instigate wherever there is no law and order. Paul says, "Anyone who does not provide for his own family denies the faith and is worse than an unbeliever" (1 Tm 5:8). On the other hand, if in great weakness they flee but provide capable substitutes to make sure that the community is well governed and protected, as we previously indicated, and if they continually and carefully supervise them [i.e., the substitutes], all that would be proper.

What applies to these two offices [Church and state] should also apply to persons who stand in a relationship of service or duty toward one another. A servant should not leave his master nor a maid her mistress except with the knowledge and permission of master or mistress. Again, a master should not desert his servant or a lady her maid unless suitable provision for their care has been made somewhere. In all these matters it is a divine command that servants and maids should render obedience and by the same token masters and ladies should take care of their servants (cf. Eph 6:5-9). Likewise, fathers and mothers are bound by God's law to serve and help their children, and children their fathers and mothers. Likewise, paid public servants such as city physicians, city clerks and constables, or whatever their titles, should not flee unless they furnish capable substitutes who are acceptable to their employer.

In the case of children who are orphaned, guardians or close friends are under obligation either to stay with them or to arrange diligently for other nursing care for their sick friends. Yes, no one should dare leave his neighbor unless there are others who will take care of the sick in their stead and nurse them. In such cases we must respect the word of Christ, "I was sick and you did not visit me" (Mt 25:41-46). According to this passage we are bound to each other in such a way that we may not forsake others in their distress but are obliged to assist and help them as we ourselves would like to be helped (cf. Mt 7:12).

Private Opinions

Where no such emergency exists and where enough people are available for nursing and taking care of the sick, and where, voluntarily or by orders, those who are weak in faith make provision so that there is no need for additional helpers, or where the sick do not want them and have refused their services, I judge that they have an equal choice either to flee or to remain. If someone is sufficiently bold and strong in faith, let him or her stay in God's name; that is certainly no sin. If someone is weak and fearful, let him or her flee in God's name as long as they do not neglect their duty toward their neighbors but have made adequate provision for others to provide nursing care. To flee from death and to save one's life is a natural tendency, implanted by God and not forbidden unless it be against God and neighbor, as Paul says in Ephesians 5:29, "No one ever hates his or her own flesh, but nourishes and cherishes it." It is even commanded that everyone should as much as possible preserve body and life and not neglect them, as Paul says in 1 Corinthians 12:21-26 that God has so ordered the members of the body that each one cares and works for the other. . . .

Examples in holy scripture abundantly prove that to flee from death is not wrong in itself. Abraham was a great saint but he feared death and escaped it by pretending that his wife, Sarah, was his sister (Gn 12:13). Because he did so without neglecting or adversely affecting his neighbor, it was not counted as a sin against him. His son, Isaac, did likewise (Gn 26:7). Jacob also fled from his brother Esau to avoid death at his hands (cf. Gn 27:43-45). Likewise, David fled from Saul, and from Absalom (cf. 1 Sm 19:10-17; 2 Sm 15:14). The prophet Uriah escaped from King Jehoiakim and fled into Egypt (Jer 26:21). The valiant prophet Elijah had destroyed all the prophets of Baal by his great faith, but afterward, when Queen Jezebel threatened him, he became afraid and fled into the desert (cf. 1 Kgs 19:3). Before that, Moses fled into the land of Midian when the king searched for him in Egypt (cf. Ex 2:15). If it is permissible to flee from one or the other in clear conscience, why not from all four? Our examples demonstrate how the holy fathers escaped from the sword; it is quite evident that Abraham, Isaac, and Jacob fled from the other scourge, namely, hunger and death, when they went to Egypt to escape famine, as we are told in Genesis (40-47). Likewise, why should one not run away from wild beasts? I hear people say, "If war or the Turks come, one should not flee from one's village or town but stay and await God's punishment by the sword." That is quite true; let those who have a strong faith wait for their death, but they should not condemn those who take flight.

By such reasoning, when a house is on fire, no one should run outside or rush to help because such a fire is also a punishment from God. Anyone who falls into deep water dare not save himself by swimming but must surrender to the water as to a divine punishment. Very well, do so if you can, but do not tempt God, and allow others to do as much as they are capable of doing. Likewise, if someone breaks a leg, is wounded or bitten, he or she should not seek medical aid but say, "It is God's punishment. I shall bear it until it heals by itself." Freezing weather and winter are also God's punishment and can cause death. Why run to get inside or near a fire? Be strong and stay outside until it becomes warm again. We should then need no apothecaries or drugs or physicians because all illnesses are punishment from God. Hunger and thirst are also great punishments and torture. Why do you eat and drink instead of letting yourself be punished until hunger and thirst stop of themselves? Ultimately such talk will lead to the point where we abbreviate the Lord's Prayer and no longer pray, "deliver us from evil, Amen," since we would have to stop praying to be saved from hell and stop seeking to escape it. It, too, is God's punishment as is every kind of evil. Where would all this end?

Prayer and Service

From what has been said we derive this guidance: We must pray against every form of evil and guard against it to the best of our ability in order not to act contrary to God, as was previously explained. If it be God's will that evil come upon us and destroy us, none of our precautions will help us. . . .

In the same way we must and we owe it to our neighbors to accord them the same treatment in other troubles and perils, also. . . .

It would be well, where there is such an efficient government in cities and states, to maintain municipal homes and hospitals staffed with people to take care of the sick so that patients from private homes can be sent there—as was the intent and purpose of our forefathers with so many pious bequests, hospices, hospitals, and infirmaries so that it should not be necessary for every citizen to maintain a hospital in the home. That would indeed be a fine, commendable, and Christian arrangement to which everyone should offer generous help and contributions, particularly the government. Where there are no such institutions—and they exist in only a few places—we must give hospital care and be nurses for one another in any extremity or risk the loss of salvation and the grace of God. Thus it is written in God's word and command, "Love your neighbor as yourself," and in Matthew 7:12, "So whatever you wish that others would do to you, do so to them."

Now if a deadly epidemic strikes, we should stay where we are, make our preparations, and take courage in the fact that we are mutually bound together (as previously indicated) so that we cannot desert one another or flee from one another. . . .

But whoever serves the sick for the sake of God's gracious promise, though they may accept a suitable reward to which they are entitled, inasmuch as every laborer is worthy of his hire—whoever does so has the great assurance that he or she shall in turn be cared for. God himself shall be their attendant and their physician, too. What an attendant he is! What a physician! Friend, what are all the physicians, apothecaries, and attendants in comparison to God? Should that not encourage one to go and serve the sick, even though they might have as many contagious boils on them as hairs on their body, and though they might be bent double carrying a hundred plague-ridden bodies?

Therefore, dear friends, let us not become so desperate as to desert our own, whom we are duty-bound to help, and flee in such a cowardly way from the terror of the devil, or allow him the joy of mocking us and vexing and distressing God and all his angels.

This I well know, that if it were Christ or his mother who were laid low by illness, everybody would be so solicitous and would gladly become a servant or helper. Everyone would want to be bold and fearless; nobody would flee but everyone would come running. And yet they don't hear what Christ himself says, "As you did to one of the least, you did it to me" (Mt 25:40). When he speaks of the greatest commandment he says, "The other commandment is like unto it, you shall love your neighbor as yourself" (Mt 22:39). There you hear that the command to love your neighbor is equal to the greatest commandment to love God, and that what you do or fail to do for your neighbor means doing the same to God. If you wish to serve Christ and to wait on him, very well, you have your sick neighbor close at hand. . . .

Realistic Care

If we make no use of intelligence or medicine when we could do so without detriment to our neighbor, we injure our body and must beware lest we become a suicide in God's eyes. By the same reasoning people might forgo eating and drinking, clothing and shelter, and boldly proclaim their faith that if God wanted to preserve them from starvation and cold, he could do so without food and clothing. Actually that would be suicide. It is even more shameful for people to pay no heed to their own body and to fail to protect it against the plague the best they are able, and then to infect and poison others who might have remained alive if they had taken care of their body as they should have. They are thus responsible before God for their neighbor's death and are murderers many times over. Indeed, such people behave as though a house were burning in the city and nobody were trying to put the fire out. Instead they give leeway to the flames so that the whole city is consumed, saying that if God so willed, he could save the city without water to quench the fire.

No, my dear friends, that is no good. Use medicine; take potions which can help you; fumigate house, yard, and street; shun persons and places wherever your neighbor does not need your presence or has recovered, and act like a person who wants to help put out the burning city. What else is the epidemic but a fire which instead of consuming wood and straw devours life and body? . . .

Moreover, those who have contracted the disease and recovered should keep away from others and not admit them into their presence unless it be necessary. Though one should aid them in times of need, as previously pointed out, they in turn should, after their recovery, so act toward others that no one becomes unnecessarily endangered on their account and so cause another's death. "Whoever loves danger," says the wise man, "will perish by it" (Eccl 3:26). If the people in a city were to show themselves bold in their faith when a neighbor's need so demands, and cautious when no emergency exists, and if everyone would help ward off contagion as best they can, then the death toll would indeed be moderate.

Miscarriage

Miscarriage was a medieval evil. It killed numerous babies and often young mothers. Families worried about the spiritual state of the aborted babies. Would they be "saved" even though they had not been baptized? Was it the fault of mothers that they died? Little, if anything, could be done if birthing became complicated due to the position of the baby in the womb, or other difficulties for which there was not yet any medical solution. Luther thought of providing a pastoral opinion on miscarriage after he read an interpretation of Psalm 29 by his friend and colleague John Bugenhagen, who was the pastor at the Town Church and a professor in Wittenberg. Luther noticed a reference to "little children" in the text and told Bugenhagen to append a piece on miscarriage. When Bugenhagen declined, Luther wrote it as an appendix. It appeared in 1542 with Bugenhagen's commentary under the title "Comfort for Women Who Have a Miscarriage." Later it was added to the collection of Luther's works. The selection is from the 1542 German edition. (Source: LW 43:247-50.)

It often happens that devout parents, particularly the wives, have sought consolation from us because they have suffered such agony and heartbreak in child-bearing when, despite their best intentions and against their will, there was a premature birth or miscarriage and their child died at birth or was born dead.

One ought not to frighten or sadden such mothers by harsh words, because it was not due to their carelessness or neglect that the birth of the child went off badly. One must make a distinction between them and those females who resent being pregnant, deliberately neglect their child, or go so far as to strangle or destroy it. This is how one ought to comfort them.

First, inasmuch as one cannot and ought not know the hidden judgment of God in such a case—why, after every possible care had been taken, God did not allow the child to be born alive and be baptized—these mothers should calm themselves and have faith that God's will is always better than ours, though it may seem otherwise to us from our human point of view. They should be confident that God is not angry with them or with others who are involved. Rather is this a test to develop patience. We well know that these cases have never been rare since the beginning and that scripture also cites them as examples, as in Psalm 58:8, and Paul calls himself an *abortivum*, a misbirth or one untimely born (cf. 1 Cor 15:8).

Second, because the mother is a believing Christian it is to be hoped that her heartfelt cry and deep longing to bring her child to be baptized will be accepted by God as an effective prayer. It is true that a Christian in deepest despair does not dare to name, wish, or hope for the help (as it seems to him or her) which he or she would wholeheartedly and gladly purchase with his or her own life were that possible, and in doing so thus find comfort. However, the words of Paul properly apply here: "Likewise the Spirit helps us in our weakness; for we do not know how to pray as we ought (that is, as was said above, we dare not express our wishes), rather the Spirit himself intercedes for us mightily with sighs too deep for words. And he who searches the heart knows what is the mind of the spirit" (Rom 8:26-27), etc. Also Ephesians 3:20, "Now to him who by the power at work within us is able to do far more abundantly than all that we ask or think."

One should not despise Christian persons as if they were pagans or godless persons. They are precious in God's sight and their prayer is powerful and great, for they have been sanctified by Christ's blood and anointed with the Spirit of God. Whatever they sincerely pray for, especially in the unexpressed yearning of their hearts, becomes a great, unbearable cry in God's ears. God must listen, as he did to Moses, "Why do you cry to me?" (Ex 14:15), even though Moses couldn't whisper, so great was his anxiety and trembling in the terrible troubles that beset him. His sighs and the deep cry of his heart divided the Red Sea and dried it up, led the children of Israel across, and drowned Pharaoh with all his army (cf. Ex 14:26-28), etc. This and even more can be accomplished by a true, spiritual longing. Even Moses did not know how or for what he should pray—not knowing how the deliverance would be accomplished—but his cry came from his heart.

Isaiah did the same against King Sennacherib (cf. Is 37:4) and so did many other kings and prophets, who accomplished inconceivable and impossible things by prayer, to their astonishment afterward. But before that they would not have dared to expect or wish so much of God. This means to receive things far higher and greater than we can understand or pray for, as Paul says in Ephesians 3:20. Again, Augustine declared that his mother was praying, sighing, and weeping for him, but did not desire anything more than that he might be converted from the errors of the Manicheans and become a Christian. Thereupon God gave her not only what she desired but, as Augustine puts it, her "chiefest desire" that is, what she longed for with unutterable sighs—that Augustine become not only a Christian but also a teacher above all others in Christendom.[1] Next to the apostles Christendom has none that is his equal.

Who can doubt that those Israelite children who died before they could be circumcised on the eighth day were yet saved by the prayers of their parents in view of the promise that God willed to be their God. God (they say) has not limited his power to the sacraments, but has made a covenant with us through his word. Therefore we ought to speak differently and in a more consoling way with Christians than with pagans or wicked people (the two are the same), even in such cases where we do not know God's hidden judgment. For he says and is not lying, "All things are possible to one who believes" (Mk 9:23), even though they have not prayed, or expected, or hoped for what they would have wanted to see happen. Enough has been said about this. Therefore one must leave such situations to God and take comfort in the thought that he surely has heard our unspoken yearning and done all things better than we could have asked.

---

1. Augustine subsequently became bishop of Hippo. His thinking has played a significant role in Christian theology and had considerable influence upon Luther, who frequently quoted from his writings.

In summary, see to it that above all else you are a true Christian and that you teach a heartfelt yearning and praying to God in true faith, be it in this or any other trouble. Then do not be dismayed or grieved about your child or yourself, and know that your prayer is pleasing to God and that God will do everything much better than you can comprehend or desire. "Call upon me," he says in Psalm 50:15, "in the day of trouble; I will deliver you, and you shall glorify me." For this reason one ought not straightway condemn such infants for whom and concerning whom believers and Christians have devoted their longing and yearning and praying. Nor ought one to consider them the same as others for whom no faith, prayer, or yearning are expressed on the part of Christians and believers. God intends that his promise and our prayer or yearning which is grounded in that promise should not be disdained or rejected, but be highly valued and esteemed. I have said it before and preached it often enough: God accomplishes much through the faith and longing of another, even a stranger, even though there is still no personal faith. But this is given through the channel of another's intercession, as in the gospel Christ raised the widow's son at Nain because of the prayers of his mother apart from the faith of the son (cf. Lk 7:11-17). And he freed the little daughter of the Canaanite woman from the demon through the faith of the mother apart from the daughter's faith (cf. Mt 15:22-28). The same was true of the king's son (Jn 4:46-53), and of the paralytic and many others of whom we need not say anything here.

How to Die

Death and dying are obligatory topics of Christian spiritual formation and pastoral care. Luther was asked to counsel his friend George Spalatin, the court chaplain of Elector Frederick the Wise, about depressing thoughts of death. The request came when Luther was busy preparing for his first decisive debate on reform proposals in Leipzig in the summer of 1519. Luther interrupted his intensive preparations for the debate to write "A Sermon on Preparing to Die" for Spalatin. In it he offers concrete pastoral advice, including the discipline of "imaging," which has found some use in modern psychotherapy. The sermon became very popular and appeared in twenty-two editions within three years, followed by others later. (Source: LW 42:99-115.)

Self-Examination

Since death marks a farewell from this world and all its activities, it is necessary that we regulate our temporal goods properly or as we wish to have them ordered, lest after our death there be occasion for squabbles, quarrels, or other misunderstanding among our surviving friends. This pertains to the physical or external departure from this world and to the surrender of our possessions.

We must also take leave spiritually. That is, we must cheerfully and sincerely forgive, for God's sake, all people who have offended us. At the same time we must also, for God's sake, earnestly seek the forgiveness of all the people whom we undoubtedly have greatly offended by setting them a bad example or by bestowing too few of the kindnesses demanded by the law of Christian love of neighbor. This is necessary lest the soul remain burdened by its actions here on earth.

Since everyone must depart, we must turn our eyes to God, to whom the path of death leads and directs us. Here we find the beginning of the narrow gate and of the straight path to life (Mt 7:14). All must joyfully venture forth on this path, for though the gate is quite narrow, the path is not long. Just as an

174

infant is born with peril and pain from the small abode of its mother's womb into this immense heaven and earth, that is, into this world, so we depart this life through the narrow gate of death. And although the heavens and the earth in which we dwell at present seem large and wide to us, they are nevertheless much narrower and smaller than the mother's womb in comparison with the future heaven. Therefore, the death of the dear saints is called a new birth, and their feast day is known in Latin as *natale*, that is, the day of their birth.[1] However, the narrow passage of death makes us think of this life as expansive and the life beyond as confined. Therefore, we must believe this and learn a lesson from the physical birth of a child, as Christ declares, "When a woman is in travail she has sorrow; but when she has recovered, she no longer remembers the anguish, since a child is born by her into the world" (Jn 16:21). So it is that in dying we must bear this anguish and know that a large mansion and joy will follow (Jn 14:2).

Such preparation and readiness for this journey are accomplished first of all by providing ourselves with a sincere confession (of at least the greatest sins and those which by diligent search can be recalled by our memory), with the holy Christian sacrament of the holy and true body of Christ, and with the unction.[2] If these can be had, one should devoutly desire them and receive them with great confidence. If they cannot be had, our longing and yearning for them should nevertheless be a comfort and we should not be too dismayed by this circumstance. Christ says, "All things are possible to him who believes" (Mk 9:23). The sacraments are nothing else than signs which help and incite us to faith, as we shall see. Without this faith they serve no purpose.

---

1. *Natale* (usually spelled *natalis*) dates back to the second century and was observed originally with a religious service commemorating a relative on the anniversary of his death. In the course of time the observance commemorated especially saints and martyrs.

2. Extreme Unction, one of the seven sacraments of the Roman Catholic Church, is administered to the gravely ill, the dying, or the just deceased. At this point Luther did not openly reject the nonscriptural sacraments.

We must earnestly, diligently, and highly esteem the holy sacraments, hold them in honor, freely and cheerfully rely on them, and so balance them against sin, death, and hell that they will outweigh these by far. We must occupy ourselves much more with the sacraments and their virtues than with our sins. However, we must know how to give them due honor, and we must know what their virtues are. I show them due honor when I believe that I truly receive what the sacraments signify and all that God declares and indicates in them, so that I can say with Mary in firm faith, "Let it be to me according to your words and signs" (Lk 1:38). Since God himself here speaks and acts through the priest, we would do him in his word and work no greater dishonor than to doubt whether it is true. And we can do him no greater honor than to believe that his word and work are true and to firmly rely on them.

We should familiarize ourselves with death during our lifetime, inviting death into our presence when it is still at a distance and not on the move. At the time of dying, however, this is hazardous and useless, for then death looms large of its own accord. In that hour we must put the thought of death out of mind and refuse to see it, as we shall hear. The power and might of death are rooted in the fearfulness of our nature and in our untimely and undue viewing and contemplating of it.

Imaging a New Life

Sin also grows large and important when we dwell on it and brood over it too much. This is increased by the fearfulness of our conscience, which is ashamed before God and accuses itself terribly. . . .

This is true especially since people feel that they should think of their sins at that time and that it is right and useful for them to engage in such contemplation. But they find themselves so unprepared and unfit that now even all their good works are turned into sins. As a result, this must lead to an unwillingness to die, disobedience to the will of God, and eternal damnation.

That is not the fitting time to meditate on sin. That must be done during one's lifetime. Thus the evil spirit turns everything upside down for us. During our lifetime, when we should constantly have our eyes fixed on the image of death, sin, and hell—as we read in Psalm 51:3, "My sin is ever before me"—the devil closes our eyes and hides these images. But in the hour of death when our eyes should see only life, grace, and salvation, he at once opens our eyes and frightens us with these untimely images so that we shall not see the true ones.

Hell also looms large because of undue scrutiny and stern thought devoted to it out of season. This is increased immeasurably by our ignorance of God's counsel. The evil spirit prods the soul so that it burdens itself with all kinds of useless presumptions, especially with the most dangerous undertaking of delving into the mystery of God's will to ascertain whether one is "chosen" or not. . . .

What is my desire to know whether I am chosen other than a presumption to know all that God knows and to be equal with him so that he will know no more than I do? Thus God is no longer God with a knowledge surpassing mine. . . .

When people are assailed by thoughts regarding their election, they are being assailed by hell, as the psalms lament so much (cf. Ps 65:4; 78; 106:4-5). Who surmounts this temptation has vanquished sin, hell, and death all in one.

In this affair we must exercise all diligence not to open our homes to any of these images and not to paint the devil over the door. These foes will of themselves boldly rush in and seek to occupy the heart completely with their image, their arguments, and their signs. And when that happens people are doomed and God is entirely forgotten. The only thing to do with these pictures at that time is to combat and expel them. Indeed, where they are found alone and not in conjunction with other pictures, they belong nowhere else than in hell among the devils.

But who wants to fight against them and drive them out will find that it is not enough just to wrestle and tussle and scuffle with them. They will prove too strong for him, and matters will go from bad to worse. The one and only approach is to drop them entirely and have nothing to do with them. But how is that done? It is done in this way: You must look at death while you are alive and see sin in the light of grace and hell in the light of heaven, permitting nothing to divert you from that view. Adhere to that even if all angels, all creatures, yes, even your own thoughts, depict God in a different light—something these will not do. It is only the evil spirit who lends that impression.

You must not view or ponder death as such, not in yourself or in your nature, nor in those who were killed by God's wrath and were overcome by death. If you do that you will be lost and defeated with them. But you must resolutely turn your gaze, the thoughts of your heart, and all your senses away from this picture and look at death closely and untiringly only as seen in those who died in God's grace and who have overcome death, particularly in Christ and then also in all his saints.

In such pictures death will not appear terrible and gruesome. No, it will seem contemptible and dead, slain and overcome in life. For Christ is nothing other than sheer life, as his saints are likewise. The more profoundly you impress that image upon your heart and gaze upon it, the more the image of death will pale and vanish of itself without struggle or battle. Thus your heart will be at peace and you will be able to die calmly in Christ and with Christ. . . .

You must not look at sin in sinners, or in your conscience, or in those who abide in sin to the end and are damned. If you do, you will surely follow them and also be overcome. You must turn your thoughts away from that and look at sin only within the picture of grace. Engrave that picture in yourself with all your power and keep it before your eyes. The picture of grace is nothing else but that of Christ on the cross and of all his dear saints.

How is that to be understood? Grace and mercy are there where Christ on the cross takes your sin from you, bears it for you, and destroys it. To believe this firmly, to keep it before your eyes and not to doubt it, means to view the picture of Christ and to engrave it in yourself. Likewise, all the saints who suffer and die in Christ also bear your sins and suffer and labor for you, as we find it written, "Bear one another's burdens and thus fulfill the command of Christ" (Gal 6:2). Christ himself exclaims in Matthew 11:28, "Come to me, all who labor and are heavy-laden, and I will help you." In this way you may view your sins in safety without tormenting your conscience. Here sins are never sins, for here they are overcome and swallowed up in Christ. . . .

So then, gaze at the heavenly picture of Christ, who descended into hell (1 Pt 3:19) for your sake and was forsaken by God as one eternally damned when he spoke the words on the cross, "Eli, Eli, lama sabachthani!"—"My God, my God, why hast thou forsaken me?" (Mt 27:46). In that picture your hell is defeated and your uncertain election is made sure. If you concern yourself solely with that and believe that it was done for you, you will surely be preserved in this same faith. Never, therefore, let this be erased from your vision. Seek yourself only in Christ and not in yourself and you will find yourself in him eternally. . . .

Sacramental Nurture

We now turn to the holy sacraments and their blessings to learn to know their benefits and how to use them. Anyone who is granted the time and the grace to confess, to be absolved, and to receive the sacrament and Extreme Unction before his or her death has great cause indeed to love, praise, and thank God and to die cheerfully, if he or she relies firmly on and believes in the sacraments, as we said earlier. In the sacraments your God, Christ himself, deals, speaks, and works with you through the priest. His are not the works and words of people. In the sacraments God himself grants you all the blessings we just mentioned in connection with Christ. God wants the sacraments to be a sign and testimony that Christ's life has taken your death, his obedience your sin, his love your hell, upon themselves and overcome them. Moreover, through the same sacraments you are included and made one with all the saints. You thereby enter into the true communion of saints so that they die with you in Christ, bear sin, and vanquish hell. . . .

It is of utmost importance that we highly esteem, honor, and rely upon the holy sacraments, which contain nothing but God's words, promises, and signs. This means that we have no doubts about the sacraments or the things of which they are certain signs, for if we doubt these we lose everything. Christ says that it will happen to us as we believe (Mt 15:28, 21). What will it profit you to assume and to believe that sin, death, and hell are overcome in Christ for others, but not to believe that your sin, your death, and your hell are also vanquished and wiped out and that you are thus redeemed? Under those circumstances the sacraments will be completely fruitless, since you do not believe the things which are indicated, given, and promised there to you. That is the vilest sin that can be committed, for God himself is looked upon as a liar in his word, signs, and works, as one who speaks, shows, and promises something which he neither means nor intends to keep. Therefore we dare not trifle with the sacraments. Faith must be present for a firm reliance and cheerful venturing on such signs and promises of God. What sort of a God or Savior would he be who could not or would not save us from sin, death, and hell? Whatever the true God promises and effects must be something big. . . .

We must note that those who receive the sacraments have a great advantage, for they have received a sign and a promise from God with which they can exercise and strengthen their belief that they have been called into Christ's image and to his benefits. The others who must do without these signs labor solely in faith and must obtain these benefits with the desires of their hearts. They will, of course, also receive these benefits if they persevere in that same faith. Thus you must also say with regard to the sacrament of the altar, "If the priest gave me the holy body of Christ, which is a sign and promise of the communion of all angels and saints that they love me, provide and pray for me, suffer and die with me, bear my sin and overcome hell, it will and must therefore be true that the divine sign does not deceive me. I will not let anyone rob me of it. I would rather deny all the world and myself than doubt my God's trustworthiness and truthfulness in his signs and promises. Whether worthy or unworthy of him, I am, according to the text and the declaration of this sacrament, a member of Christendom. It is better that I be unworthy than that God's truthfulness be questioned. Devil, away with you if you advise me differently...."

The right use of the sacraments involves nothing more than believing that all will be as the sacraments promise and pledge through God's word. Therefore, it is necessary not only to look at the three pictures in Christ and with these to drive out the counterpictures, but also to have a definite sign which assures us that this has surely been given to us. That is the function of the sacraments.

In the hour of death no Christian should doubt that he or she is not alone. We can be certain, as the sacraments point out, that a great many eyes are upon us: first, the eyes of God and of Christ himself, for the Christian believes his words and clings to his sacraments; then also, the eyes of the dear angels, of the saints, and of all Christians. There is no doubt, as the sacrament of the altar indicates, that all of these in a body run to us as one of their own, help us overcome sin, death, and hell, and bear all things with us. In that hour the work of love and the communion of saints are seriously and mightily active. Christians must see this for themselves and have no doubt regarding it, for then they will be bold in death. Who doubts this does not believe in the most venerable sacrament of the Body of Christ, in which are pointed out, promised, and pledged the communion, help, love, comfort, and support of all the saints in all times of need....

Prayer

Let us not presume to perform such things by our own power, but humbly ask God to create and preserve such faith in and such understanding of his holy sacraments in us. We must practice awe and humility in all this, lest we ascribe these works to ourselves instead of allowing God the glory. . . .

God has enjoined us firmly to believe in the fulfillment of our prayer (Mk 11:24). We must also bring this command of God to his attention and say, "My God, you have commanded me to pray and to believe that my prayer will be heard. For this reason I come to you in prayer and am assured that you will not forsake me but will grant me a genuine faith."

Moreover, we should implore God and his dear saints our whole life long for true faith in the last hour. . . .

When the hour of death is at hand we must offer prayer to God and, in addition, remind him of his command and of his promise and not doubt that our prayer will be fulfilled. After all, if God commanded us to pray and to trust in prayer, and, furthermore, has granted us the grace to pray, why should we doubt that his purpose in this was also to hear and to fulfill it?

What more should God do to persuade you to accept death willingly and not to dread but to overcome it? In Christ he offers you the image of life, of grace, and of salvation so that you may not be horrified by the images of sin, death, and hell. Furthermore, he lays your sin, your death, and your hell on his dearest Son, vanquishes them, and renders them harmless for you. In addition, he lets the trials of sin, death, and hell that come to you also assail his Son and teaches you how to preserve yourself in the midst of these and how to make them harmless and bearable. And to relieve you of all doubt, he grants you a sure sign, namely, the holy sacraments. He commands his angels, all saints, all creatures to join him in watching over you, to be concerned about your soul, and to receive it. He commands you to ask him for this and to be assured of fulfillment. What more can or should he do?

From this you can see that he is a true God and that he performs great, right, and divine works for you. Why, then, should he not impose something big upon you (such as dying), as long as he adds to it great benefits, help, and strength, and thereby wants to test the power of his grace? Thus we read in

Psalm 111:2, "Great are the works of the Lord, selected according to his pleasure." Therefore, we ought to thank him with a joyful heart for showing us such wonderful, rich, and immeasurable grace and mercy against death, hell, and sin, and to laud and love his grace rather than fearing death so greatly. Love and praise make dying very much easier.

Wit
and
Witness

Table Talk

Luther often mixed faith and humor when he encountered haughty minds who needed to be ridiculed, or in his pastoral care for timid souls who needed help. Selections 17-23 offer samples of Luther's use of humor. The first six selections have been culled from the massive edition of "table talks," the final one from the voluminous correspondence. Luther and his spouse Katie (Catharina von Bora) scheduled the main meal of the day early in the evening to have time for students and other guests after the meal. They lived in the Augustinian monastery in Wittenberg where Luther had been an anxious monk. The monastery had been given to Luther as a wedding gift by Elector Frederick the Wise in 1525. "Table talks" were recorded by students and friends who often enjoyed the generous hospitality of the Luther parsonage.

Dogs and Prayer

When Luther's puppy happened to be at the table, looked for a morsel from his master, and watched with open mouth and motionless eyes, he [Martin Luther] said, "Oh, if I could only pray the way this dog watches the meat! All his thoughts are concentrated on the piece of meat. Otherwise he has no thought, wish, or hope."

Behold, the heart of the pious dog was also lacking in this, that he could not pray without thoughts.

The Purpose of Mice

On March 18 [1539] some field mice broke into his [Martin Luther's] house and gnawed to pieces his best ornamental branches of fruit trees and laurels. He was quite annoyed. In a short time he caught a mouse in a mousetrap. It was almost as large as a dormouse, but with a bigger head, a shorter tail, and rather long teeth. When he had looked at it he said, "It looks like a beaver, which can also cut down trees. It has done me harm, but it has paid for it with the highest price."

That same day his wife drowned many mice in some holes in the garden. He [Martin Luther] said, "Mice also serve a useful purpose, for they make diligent housefathers. It's as Augustine said about heretics, that they have the function of inciting and provoking Catholics and theologians not to be so cool toward the word of God; when the opportunity is met, they begin to boil. It happened so to me.

How to Preach

Conrad Cordatus said to Dr. Martin Luther, "Reverend Father, teach me in a brief way how to preach."

Luther responded briefly, "First, you must learn to go up to the pulpit. Second, you must know that you should stay there for a time. Third, you must learn to get down again."

He added nothing in addition to these words, and as a result Cordatus was quite angry. Yet at length it occurred to him that the doctor had hit the mark very well. Anybody who keeps this order will be a good preacher. First, he must learn to go up to the pulpit, that is, he should have a regular and a divine call. Second, he must learn to stay there for a time, that is, he should have the pure and genuine doctrine. Third, he must also learn to get down again, that is, he should preach not more than an hour.

Writing Mania

Printers in Augsburg and Wittenberg urged Luther to allow them to publish his collected works. He replied, "I'll never consent to this proposal of yours. I'd rather that all my books would disappear and the holy scriptures alone would be read. Otherwise we'll rely on such writings and let the Bible go. Brenz wrote such a big commentary on twelve chapters of Luke that it disgusts the reader to look into it. The same is true of my commentary on Galatians. I wonder who encourages this mania for writing! Who wants to buy such stout tomes? And if they're bought, who'll read them? And if they're read, who'll be edified by them?"

What God Did Before the Creation

Severus said, "The scholastics even disputed about the question of where God was before the creation of the world. I heard Camers reply in Vienna that God was in himself."

The doctor [Martin Luther] said, "Yes, Augustine mentioned this. But once, when he was asked, he said, 'God was making hell for those who are inquisitive.' " Then he added, "Where is God now, after the creation?"

Letter from the Grave

A certain messenger came from Hall, in the valley of the Inn in the Alps. He informed Dr. Martin [Luther] about a very common rumor in Italy . . . to the effect that Martin Luther was dead and buried and that his epitaph was written in Hebrew, Greek, and Latin letters. Many godly people were saddened by this rumor, the messenger said, and requested him to bring them a copy of the epitaph. "Since I find Your Reverence still alive," he said, "I beg you to give me a letter from your grace in order that with it I may comfort the godly people who have been grieving."

Dr. Martin [Luther] smiled and said, "This is an extraordinary request. Never before in my life have I written anything from my grave!" Nevertheless he wrote the following lines: "I, Dr. Martin Luther, testify herewith in my own hand that I am of one mind with all my enemies, for they wish to rejoice over my death. I begrudge them their joy from the bottom of my heart and would willingly have died but God was not yet ready to sanction such joy. He will do this, however, sooner than they think, and it will be their misfortune, for they will then say, 'Would that Luther were still alive!' This is a transcript in German, Greek, Latin, and Hebrew from my grave."

Last Letter to Katie

Grace and peace in Christ! Most holy Mrs. Doctor! I thank you very kindly for your great worry which robs you of sleep. Since the date that you [started to] worry about me, the fire in my quarters, right outside the door of my room, tried to devour me, and yesterday, no doubt because of the strength of your worries, a stone almost fell on my head and nearly squashed me as in a mousetrap. For in our secret chamber [toilet] mortar has been falling down for about two days; we called in some people who [merely] touched the stone with two fingers and it fell down. The stone was as big as a long pillow and as wide as a large hand; it intended to repay you for your holy worries, had the dear angels not protected [me]. [Now] I worry that if you do not stop worrying the earth will finally swallow us up and all the elements will chase us. Is this the way you learned the Catechism and the faith? Pray and let God worry. You have certainly not been commanded to worry about me or about yourself. "Cast your burden on the Lord, and he will sustain you," as is written in Psalm 55:22 and many more passages.

With this I commend you to God. We would gladly be free and drive home, if God would will it. Amen.

Your Holiness' willing servant,
Martin Luther

Chronology

1483   Born 10 November in Eisleben.
1484   Family moves to Mansfeld.
1492   Attends school in Mansfeld.
1497   Sent to school in Magdeburg.
1498   Transfers to St. George School in Eisenach.
1501   Enters Erfurt University.
1502   Earns B.A. degree.
1505   Earns M.A. degree in January. Begins law studies in May. Enters monastery 17 July.
1506   Takes monastic vows.
1507   Ordained.
1508   Sent to Wittenberg to lecture on moral philosophy.
1509   Earns Biblical Baccalaureate in March. Licensed to teach the *Sentences of Lombard* in the fall. Returns to Erfurt as *Sententiarius*.
1510   Sent to Rome in November by the Order.
1511   Returns from Rome in April. Transferred to monastery in Wittenberg.
1512   Earns doctorate, October. Joins theological faculty in Wittenberg.
1513   Begins lectures on Psalms.
1515   Begins lectures on Romans. Reads John Tauler.
1516   Begins lectures on Galatians.
1517   Begins lectures on Hebrews. Criticizes sale of indulgences. Attacks scholastic theology. Publicizes Ninety-Five Theses, 31 October.
1518   Defends his stance on indulgences. Summoned to Rome. Meets with Cardinal Cajetan in Augsburg, October. Asks to be heard by council.
1519   Meets with papal emissary Miltitz, January. Debates with John Eck at Leipzig. Condemned by universities of Cologne and Louvain.
1520   Publishes major reform treatises, beginning with "To the Christian Nobility of the German Nation." Appeals to General Council. Burns papal bull in December.
1521   Condemned by bull *Decet Romanum pontificem*, January. Appears before and is condemned by Imperial Diet of Worms. Hides at the Wartburg. Begins translation of New Testament.
1522   Returns to Wittenberg, March. Responds to Henry VIII. Publishes German translation of New Testament.
1523   Initiates liturgical, educational, and social reforms in Wittenberg. Begins lectures on Deuteronomy.
1524   Begins lectures on Minor Prophets. Debates with Carlstadt on matters of social reform and the Lord's Supper.

1525 Marries Catherine von Bora, 13 June. Writes against rebellious peasants and Carlstadt. Publishes "On the Bondage of the Will" against Erasmus.

1526 Becomes father of son Hans.
Supports the organization of a Lutheran Church in Saxony.

1527 Writes against Zwingli on Lord's Supper. Experiences first severe attacks of stones and heart problems. Becomes father of daughter Elizabeth.

1528 Grieves over death of Elizabeth. Writes seminal "Confession" on Lord's Supper.

1529 Publishes Small and Large Catechisms. Becomes father of Magdalene (Lenchen). Travels to Marburg for colloquy with Zwingli.

1530 Lives in Fortress Coburg in spring and summer. His father dies.

1531 Becomes father of Martin.
Writes "Warning" to his "Dear Germans." His mother dies.

1532 Frequently ill. Meets with new elector who regards him as his "spiritual father."

1533 Becomes father of Paul. Writes on Mass and the priesthood.

1534 Becomes father of Margaret. Publishes German Bible.

1535 Presides over doctoral disputations. Meets with papal emissary Vergerio regarding a future council.

1536 Agrees to "Wittenberg Concord" on the Lord's Supper after negotiations with South German Protestants.

1537 Travels to Smalcald. Has severe stone attacks. Publishes the "Smalcald Articles" as his theological testament.

1539 Becomes involved in the antinomian controversies against John Agricola, who claimed there is no need for law among Christians.

1540 Agrees to Philip of Hesse's plan to commit bigamy.

1541 Writes vitriolic treatises against pope and Duke Henry of Brunswick. Goes on preaching tour and consecrates Nicholas Amsdorf "bishop" of Naumburg.

1542 Grieves over death of fourteen-year-old Lenchen. Drafts his will.

1543 Writes most offensive treatises against Jews.

1544 Writes against Caspar Schwenckfeld's interpretation of the Lord's Supper.

1545 Makes final revisions on Bible translation. Writes an autobiographical Preface to Latin edition of collected works.

1546 Dies in Eisleben, 18 February.
Buried in Castle Church, 22 February.

1552 Catherine von Bora dies.